THE STORY OF LIBERTY

AMERICA'S HERITAGE THROUGH THE CIVIL WAR

BY JOHN DE GREE
THE CLASSICAL HISTORIAN™

Copyright © 2017 by The Classical Historian™ All Rights Reserved.
Published by The Classical Historian™
Printed in the United States of America.

No part of this book may be used or reproduced in any manner whatsoever without written permission except in the case of a brief quotation embodied in critical articles and reviews.
Graphic Artist: Patty Roberts
Editor: Jane M. Elder
History Editor: Michael Allen

More Information: john@classicalhistorian.com
www.classicalhistorian.com

Table of Contents

Foreword v
by Michael Allen, Ph.D., University of Washington, Tacoma

Introduction 1

I. America's Ancient Heritage
Introduction 5
Chapter 1. The Fertile Crescent 9
2. The Greeks 13
3. The Roman Republic 17
4. Western Civilization 21

II. America's Medieval Heritage
Introduction 23
Chapter 5. The Age of Barbarians 25
6. Civilizing Europe 27
7. Foundation of European Kingdoms 29
8. Development of Liberty in Medieval England 31
9. The Crusades 35
10. The Age of Exploration and Christopher Columbus 37
11. The Reformation and the Enlightenment 43

III. European Colonization of America
Introduction 45
Chapter 12. Native Americans 47
13. Spanish and French Colonies in America 51
14. Founding of American Exceptionalism: Jamestown and Plymouth Plantation 55
15. American Exceptionalism Takes Hold in the English Colonies 63
16. Commonalities of Life in the English Colonies 71
17. Southern Colonies 75
18. New England Colonies 77
19. The Middle Colonies 81
20. Early Indian Wars 83

IV. Founding of the U.S.A.

Introduction		87
Chapter	21. Early Causes of the American Revolution	89
	22. Land Regulation, Taxes, and Conflict	93
	23. Moving Toward War	97
	24. The Beginning of the American Revolution	101
	25. The Declaration of Independence	105
	26. Defeat, Surprise, and Survival	113
	27. The Articles of Confederation, 1777-1789	117

V. The Constitution

Introduction		121
Chapter	28. The Making of the American Constitution	123
	29. Principles of the Constitution	129
	30. Individual Rights	133

VI. Era of the Founding Fathers, 1787-1825

Introduction		137
Chapter	31. Ratification of the Constitution	139
	32. The American People	143
	33. Father of the Country	147
	34. Presidency of John Adams (1797-1801)	155
	35. The Supreme Court, Judicial Review, and Capitalism	157
	36. Presidency of Thomas Jefferson (1801-1809)	161
	37. Presidency of James Madison (1809-1817)	167
	38. The Era of Good Feelings	171
	39. American Spirit and Industry in the Free North	173
	40. Railroads, the Post Office, and the Politicization of News	175
	41. The Missouri Compromise	179

VII. The Beginning of Big Government, 1825-1836

Introduction		181
Chapter	42. The Election of 1824 and the Presidency of John Quincy Adams	183
	43. The Age of Jackson (1828-1835)	185

VIII. Empire of Liberty or Manifest Destiny, 1836-1848

Introduction		193
Chapter	44. Change in America: Industrialization, Religion, and Social Change	195
	45. Education in Early America through the Civil War	203
	46. The Southwest and the War for Texas Independence (1835-1836)	209
	47. Presidencies of Van Buren (1837-1841), Harrison (1841), and Tyler (1841-1845)	213
	48. Presidency of Polk (1845-1849) and the Mexican-American War (1846-1848)	215
	49. The California Gold Rush and the Oregon Trail	219

IX. Sectionalism

Introduction		223
Chapter	50. The South	225
	51. The North	231
	52. Life in the West	235
	53. Immigration	239

X. The Slavery Crisis Becomes Violent, 1848-1860

Introduction		243
Chapter	54. Political Instability and the End of Westward Expansion	245
	55. The Decade Preceding the Civil War	249
	56. Abraham Lincoln	253

XI. The Civil War

Introduction		257
Chapter	57. The Election of 1860	259
	58. Secession and the Confederate States of America	261
	59. Fort Sumter and the War on Paper	263
	60. Bull Run and the Beginning of the War	267
	61. Growth of Government	271
	62. The Emancipation Proclamation	273
	63. Hard War	275
	64. Unconditional Surrender Grant and Lincoln's Reelection	281
	65. The End of the War and Lincoln's Assassination	283
	66. Winners, Losers and Lasting Changes	287

Foreword

Young American history students and their teachers have long yearned for a book like the one you now hold in your hands. John De Gree's *The Story of Liberty, America's Heritage through the Civil War,* is a well-researched, ably-written, and sensible depiction of American history from the founding through the Civil War. What do I mean by "sensible"? Simply this: De Gree relates the truth about the American past by telling about our many good qualities and accomplishments as well as the setbacks our nation has endured during its long history. Few books as good as this one have been published for young readers. At last we have a new, up-to-date book suitable for American middle school and high school history students.

When Larry Schweikart and I first published our #1 New York Times best-selling book, *A Patriot's History of the United States,* we succeeded in filling a similar void existing in college-level American history books. Larry and I have often said that American history is not the story of, to use an old folk saying, a "half-empty cup." Indeed, we argued that the American cup was nearly full. Americans have made great mistakes, but they have also done much that is good. American patriots in 1776 created a democratic republic governed by ordinary citizens at a time in history when absolutist monarchs ruled most of Europe, all-powerful Czars, Emperors, and Shoguns tyrannized Russia and the Far East, and some Middle Eastern and North African monarchs claimed divine authority and direct links to God. While it is true that Americans allowed the enslavement of African-American people, they ultimately fought a bloody war that ended slavery forever. While American soldiers killed native Indians and pushed them westward onto reservations, American diplomats signed legally binding treaties that those Indians' descendants use to their great benefit in courts today. And while there has been poverty and suffering in our country's history, it pales in comparison to that of the rest of the world. It is no accident that, for over 400 years, millions of foreigners have yearned and sought to become Americans.

John De Gree tells about this and much more in *The Story of Liberty, America's Heritage through the Civil War*. He traces our nation's past from the time of the Pilgrims through the Colonial era and the American Revolution. He explains Jeffersonian and Jacksonian politics and the critical events leading to the Civil War. And he narrates the military and political history of that pivotal conflict. De Gree has a unique way of telling the story of the United States. He places special emphasis on America's place in the history of advancing Western Civilization. He begins with our classical roots and ties to ancient Hebrew, Greek, Roman, and Western European institutions. Just as importantly, he accurately weaves the story of Christianity and Christian values into the American story. No truthful history of the United States of America can ignore this vital religious element.

I first met John De Gree nearly a decade ago when we collaborated on curriculum for the growing number of homeschool, charter, private, and public school students who utilize his Classical Historian method. I remain impressed with his intellect and work ethic, and the range of exciting, effective tools he offers modern students of American history and their teachers. I am confident *The Story of Liberty, America's Heritage through the Civil War*, will become a very successful textbook in educating a future generation of American patriots.

Michael Allen, Ph.D.
University of Washington, Tacoma, 2017

American History and
The Story of Liberty

Introduction

This book is part of a series devoted to teaching the story of liberty throughout history. Liberty means at least two things: having freedom to and having freedom not to. A goal of liberty is to provide maximum development of an individual's capacity to be human, to love, to think, to choose to be charitable, to believe in God and follow a religion or not to, to start and run a business, to have a family or to choose not to. It is the freedom an individual has to live his life to its full potential. The story of liberty is as old as the human race, and for much of our world's history, including today, the great majority of people have not lived in liberty. Only recently, within the last few hundred years, have some people enjoyed a great deal of this freedom.

In modern times, the United States of America has been the leader of liberty. This is why France gave the Statue of Liberty to the United States in the 1800s. It is why immigrants have come first to the United States of America, over other countries, since its inception in 1776. It is the reason that, even though the United States trails China and India in population by about 1.3 billion to 325 million, the U.S. has the greatest economy on Earth. Liberty is a universal idea that continues to fill the hearts and minds of people around the world.

The American Founding Fathers defined liberty in the American founding documents, the Declaration of Independence and the Constitution. Like John Locke before him, Thomas Jefferson believed liberty rested on the principles that "all men are created equal," and "that they are endowed by their Creator with certain unalienable Rights, that among these are Life, Liberty, and the pursuit of Happiness." The founders believed that the rights of Americans rested on the idea that the Creator formed man with rights that no government had the authority to remove. God existed as the authority above government, above man, and the government was always subject to uphold and defend the rights given to man by the Creator. Jefferson and the other Founders fought Great Britain to establish a limited government so that individuals would have maximum freedom.

In the Constitution, liberty is defined in the Bill of Rights, the first ten amendments. The First Amendment guarantees the right to free speech, freedom of the press, religious freedom, and the right to assemble. The founders were very concerned about freedom of political speech, meaning the right to campaign or financially support the candidate of one's choice without limitation. They wanted to make sure that government would never become so strong that it would limit Americans' ability to participate in politics. Regarding freedom of religion, the founders wanted to make sure the government would not enforce a state religion, however, at the same time, they wanted Americans to never be limited in their practice of religious worship. There are other important rights in the first ten amendments, such as the right to bear arms, and the right to be free from unreasonable searches and seizures. However, the main point of the Bill of Rights was to make sure that government would never take away the liberty of Americans.

The story of liberty is the story of Western Civilization. It begins with early man, develops over the centuries, and in many ways, it comes to fruition with the birth of America. In ancient times, most humans on Earth believed in many gods; leaders imposed unfair laws on their subjects; and life was short and miserable for those without power. Unfortunately, this remains the case in some places today. However, about 4,000 years ago, the Hebrews believed in one God, in justice, and in morality, regardless of the circumstance of one's birth. Then, around 2,500 years ago, the ancient Athenians created democracy, the idea that citizens had the right to vote for their leaders and laws and not be subject to a king. At about the same time, the Romans established a republic. Citizens had rights the government had to respect. As the Roman Republic spread, liberty increased.

In 27 B.C., the Roman Empire arose and the liberties people had under the Roman Republic greatly diminished. However, within the Roman Empire, Jesus Christ established a new religious belief where God loved everyone in an equal manner. For the first time in history, a religion offered salvation to all people, not just people of a certain nationality or tribe. This religious understanding of equality under God was transformed over time into the idea that all people should be treated the same by the law. And thus, Thomas Jefferson wrote, "all men are created equal."

The story of liberty in America has not been a perfect one. From 1776 to 1865, slavery was legal in half of the country. How could a person have liberty if he were owned by another person? In addition, women were not allowed to vote and did not have the same property rights as men. From 1861 to 1865, Americans fought their greatest war, the Civil War, which resolved this paradox of liberty and slavery. Though it took 89 years, the rights Jefferson spoke about in the Declaration of Independence finally did spread to all men, black and white. In addition, throughout the 1800s and early 1900s, the political rights of women expanded to be equal with men. However, liberty in America is still not perfect. It remains today an ideal that Americans strive for.

This volume of history is the story of liberty, specifically as it relates to American history. It traces the influence of ancient and medieval civilizations on the establishment and development of the United States of America through the Civil War. It is written with the hope that young Americans will appreciate the uniqueness of America as a leader of liberty. It is these young people who are called to further the cause of liberty within our country and throughout the world.

UNIT 1

America's Ancient Heritage

Introduction

There is a very close connection between a child and parent. Parents are the people who gave us life, who feed us, who provide us a bed to sleep in, and who teach us how to brush our teeth and say "thank you." We also look like our parents, speak the same language, and we pray, or don't pray, as our parents do. In many ways, who we are depends greatly on who our parents are. If someone wanted to determine what kind of a person you would become when you get older, or what type of work you might do, he could study your parents and make some good guesses.

In the same way, a country looks very similar to the culture that founded it. The best word to describe this is heritage. Heritage means something inherited from the past. The United States of America started as 13 English colonies, originally founded by Great Britain in the 1600s. Because of this, much of America can be traced to our British heritage.

When we look at a person's past for understanding, we do not stop with studying his or her parents. We also look at grandparents, great-grandparents, and ancestors as far back in time as possible. It is the same when we study America's heritage. Even though Great Britain founded the 13 English colonies that would become the United States of America, we can trace America's heritage to thousands of years ago, to cultures and countries much older than Great Britain.

Historians divide history into different periods, or times, so that we can understand them better. Ancient history refers to the beginning of the history of man up to the end of the Western Roman Empire (A.D. 476). Medieval history begins with the end of the Roman Empire and continues until about

1500. And modern history refers to the time from about 1500 to today. Our first unit focuses on the ancient heritage of America. Although the United States of America is a modern nation, beginning with the founding of Jamestown in 1607, its heritage can be traced back to ancient times.

The United States of America is strongly influenced by the great civilizations of the Ancient Near East and northern Africa. By great, we mean that the civilizations had a large influence on future civilizations. By civilizations, we mean that these peoples had complex agricultural, urban settlements that allowed for inventions and societal developments that made life better. Early, uncivilized peoples are hunters and gatherers who roam over an area (nomads), who do not read and write, and who do not have the technology to build permanent structures. Their lives are short and they do not give much to later nations. Great civilizations, however, are marked by people who develop writing, and who pass on to others inventions or technologies that prolong or improve life. Civilized nations in the ancient world used farming technology that allowed people to have permanent homes and a consistent food supply.

The world's great early civilizations began on the banks of rivers. Ancient people who lived near rivers could fish for food, drink water, travel on boats, and use the water to irrigate their lands. Irrigate means to water fields so crops can grow. Water from large rivers allowed these people to build strong societies.

One of the beliefs of nearly all ancient people was that the world was created and ruled by many gods. There was a god for the wind, a god for the ocean, and a god for the rain. People who believe in many gods are called polytheists. Polytheists believe that if you want something, you can make a sacrifice to a god, and this god might then give it to you. If you want it to rain, you might kill an animal and burn it to make the rain god happy. Sadly, some polytheists sacrificed other humans, even children, to their gods.

Polytheists did not believe that there was a clear right and wrong. Since there were many gods, and sometimes the gods competed with each other, what was right often depended on what the ruler said was right. In Egypt, in ancient Africa, the leader was called pharaoh, and all Egyptians had to consider pharaoh a god. For the pharaoh, right was whatever made him strong. This meant that if the pharaoh believed killing someone made him strong, then killing was right.

One people of ancient times, the Hebrews, believed in one God. This idea is known as monotheism. The Hebrews believed that their God created a moral system built on what was right and what was wrong. Hebrews believed that God gave them their moral system as well as their system of laws. It is from the Hebrews that Western man received these foundations. America's laws are founded on Mosaic Law, which includes the well-known Ten Commandments.

Much of America's culture, language, laws, government, philosophy, and performing arts comes from ancient Greece and Rome. Classical Greece and Rome established democracy and representative democracy, cultural norms, and artistic practices that are exhibited in the United States of America today. The American Founding Fathers thought so highly of ancient Greece and Rome that they used the architectural styles of the Classical world, known as Neoclassicism, for the most important buildings in Washington, D.C. To appreciate American history, it is necessary to understand ancient Greece and Rome.

Within the Roman Empire, a Hebrew carpenter and his wife had a boy named Jesus who founded the first universal belief, the first religion open to all people in the world, and brought the idea of equality before God to all. This belief would have a direct role in the establishment of the United States of America. Jesus Christ taught that God loved all people in an equal manner and that salvation was open to all, regardless of one's tribe or nation. About one thousand, seven hundred and seventy-six years after the birth of Christ, Thomas Jefferson wrote in America's founding document, the Declaration of Independence, "…all men are created equal, that they are endowed by their Creator with certain unalienable Rights, that among these are Life, Liberty and the pursuit of Happiness." Jefferson linked the ancient religious beliefs of Christianity to the founding of the world's first modern republic. This heritage from ancient times shaped the United States of America that we know today.

Chapter 1

The Fertile Crescent

The Fertile Crescent is an area in the Ancient Near East, including northern Africa, and encompasses the Euphrates, Tigris, and Nile rivers. Fertile means that crops grow well because the soil is rich. Crescent refers to the visible shape of the moon when it is less than half. Interestingly, the Fertile Crescent, in the shape of a crescent moon, is where the first great civilizations began. Thus, this area is the beginning of our story of American history, because the Fertile Crescent cultural lifestyle influences us today. America's cultural ancestors came from the Fertile Crescent.

The life of a hunter and gatherer is challenging. It is hard to build a permanent home, because when the animals move, a hunter cannot move a permanent home. Thus, hunters and gatherers never created large societies. This way of life changed in Sumeria, an early advanced Fertile Crescent civilization. Sumerians developed farming on a large scale. They learned that plants grow from seeds and how to grow crops. They also developed irrigation, a system to water large areas of land so crops could grow. Their food supply was stable, and the Sumerian population grew. With this stable food supply, Sumerians did not need to roam the land, and they built permanent shelters. They also created the first written language, called cuneiform, in about 3,000 B.C. The Sumerians wrote perhaps the oldest written story, The Epic of Gilgamesh.

Other great civilizations rose and fell in the Fertile Crescent. The Babylonians developed a lunar calendar with 12 months, a 7-day week, a 24-hour day, and a 60-minute hour. King Hammurabi of Babylonia was the first to write down all laws and have them publicly displayed. "Hammurabi's Code" protected all people. Since the law was written and displayed, everyone knew what was the law and everyone had to follow it. The Hittites were one of the first peoples to make iron. The Phoenicians were a sea-going people who traveled and traded throughout the Mediterranean Sea. Phoenicians created the world's first alphabet. Later, the Latins would alter this and create the Latin alphabet, which we use today. The Latins were the people who established the Roman Republic.

Some ancient people groups of the Fertile Crescent valued reading, writing, and arithmetic. People wrote on wet clay tablets that hardened. The Assyrians had a library in Nineveh with thousands of clay tablets containing arithmetic, literature, and chemistry. The Chaldeans were the first to divide the circle into 360 degrees.

Persians and Egyptians from the Persian Empire and Ancient Egypt developed highly organized countries, bureaucratic systems, arithmetic and surveying. Egyptians made paper from papyrus, which made writing and keeping records much easier than before.

It is important to understand how laws were made and understood in most of the early civilizations of the Fertile Crescent. Supreme leaders, such as kings, chiefs and pharaohs, believed either that they were the representatives of God, or that they were one of the gods. This meant that to be a good citizen of that civilization, one had to follow exactly what the leader said. Ideas of what was right and wrong depended solely on the leader. There was no understanding of morality or justice that existed beyond the opinion of the leader. One only had to obey the leader. This meant that if the leader told a person to kill someone and the person followed through with this order, he did what was right. When the pharaoh of Egypt ordered someone killed, Egyptians took it to mean the voice of God and obeyed. Only one ancient people of the Fertile Crescent did not accept this view—the Hebrews.

THE HEBREWS

Western Civilization means the people that have certain shared ideas and beliefs. The idea of only one God, and that all people should be treated equally by the law, is part of Western Civilization. Many of these important ideas started with the Hebrews. The Hebrews were the world's first monotheists, which means they believed in only one God. Sometime between 2000 B.C. and 1600 B.C., the Hebrews believe that God spoke to one man, Abraham, and made a covenant, a special promise. God told Abraham that he would be the father of a great nation, the Hebrews. Abraham promised God that the Hebrews would be loyal to only Him. As long as the Hebrews were loyal, God told Abraham that He would protect the Hebrews. Abraham and his wife Sarah heard God and traveled from the land between the Tigris and Euphrates Rivers (Mesopotamia) all the way to Canaan, where the Hebrews later founded a country, called Israel. This is roughly in the area of the modern-day country of Israel. The Hebrews came to be called the Jews and their religion, Judaism.

The Hebrews believed one God was the Creator of all, and they believed in morality, the idea that there is a right and wrong. Hebrews taught that all people lived under God's dominion and were ruled by the same Truth. We can also call this a moral order. Sometime around 1300 B.C., God gave the Hebrews a set of laws to live by. Called the Mosaic Law, it is one of the first sets of written laws that deal with relationships (Hammurabi's Code does as well), placing importance on respecting parents and helping those in need. Have you ever heard of the Ten Commandments? They are part of the Mosaic Law.

Whereas other Fertile Crescent civilizations saw their rulers as either gods or representatives of God, the Hebrews saw their leaders as servants of God. This crucial difference between the Hebrews and other ancient civilizations has influenced great numbers of people over the last three millennia. As servants of God, Hebrews could not change the moral code established in Mosaic Law. Laws of Hebrew leaders could not be self-serving, but had to serve the God of the Mosaic Law. This idea, of a moral code established by God, which the rulers must live by and enforce, was passed onto all the cultures of Western Civilization, including the United States of America.

The government of the ancient Hebrews gives us an example of the first balanced government in the world. Balanced means that there was not one person ruling, but instead different people or groups held governmental powers. When power in government is separated, citizens have more liberty because no one person can take all the power and tell everyone else what to do. When the Hebrews conquered the Canaanites, beginning in 1407 B.C., the Hebrews were ruled by judges chosen from different tribes. From c. 1050 B.C. through 922 B.C., the Hebrews established the Kingdom of Israel. The kings did not hold ultimate power, but shared authority with prophets (messengers from God), the Torah (sacred scripture), and religious leaders.

What Americans Inherited from Countries of the Fertile Crescent

Just as a child resembles his ancestors, the United States of America resembles the ancient civilizations of the Fertile Crescent. Americans enjoy these contributions, to name just a few: written language; arithmetic; surveying; respect for books, information and libraries; technology; written law that does not change with each leader; a 12-month calendar; and a 7-day week. And, most Americans believe in morality and in one God. The people from the Fertile Crescent are not just from the distant past, unrelated to Americans. They are our cultural ancestors.

Chapter 2

THE GREEKS

Another ancient civilization that greatly influences the United States of America is Greece. On hundreds of small islands and on steep mountains with rocky soil, groups of hearty men and women established the foundations of Western Civilization. For Western Civilization, the Greek city-state of Athens stands out because of all the cultural gifts this civilization passed on.

In ancient Greece, there was no one nation of "Greece." Instead, there were a number of Greek cities, each with its own laws, customs, army, and its own way of living. Called city-states, these cities had various governments, ranging from the most democratic Athens to the militaristic Sparta. From ancient Athens, America inherited its idea of citizenship, its democratic tradition, and its love of beauty in philosophy, art, literature, and architecture. During what historians call Classical Greece (c. 5th century to 3rd century B.C.), ancient Athenians chose the system of direct democracy. In direct democracy, citizens vote directly for all laws. At the same time in the Roman Republic, Romans practiced representative democracy. In representative democracy, citizens vote for representatives who make the laws.

Ancient Greeks were fiercely independent people who ruled the Greek peninsula from about 2000 B.C. until the Romans conquered them in 146 B.C. Greece lies at the crossroads of Europe and the Ancient Near East on the Mediterranean Sea. Because of its location, Greece was the battle place for many invasions from Asia. Throughout Greece there are high mountains, countless rivers and an ever-present coast. The high mountains made it important for each city-state to be self-sufficient (to take care of itself). Because of Greece's tough environment, it is fitting that self-government began in ancient Greece.

Athens was the birthplace of both philosophy and democracy. Philosophy is the study of knowledge, truth, and the best way to live. Democracy is where each citizen votes on every law. Socrates (470-399 B.C.), the father of Western philosophy, taught Plato, who wrote that the goal in life was to pursue truth, goodness, and beauty. Athenians believed that citizens should be free, and that it was wrong to have an all-powerful king. Athenians had three branches of government—executive, legislative, judicial—with each branch having a separate job. They did this so no one Athenian would become too powerful.

In the fifth and fourth centuries B.C., Plato taught Aristotle, ancient Greece's most prolific writer on philosophy, government, and science. Aristotle believed that all people had a common human nature, that all people have reason, and that all should participate in government. He did not think there should be a certain group of special people in charge of government, but that all citizens over 18 should participate equally. (Some Athenian women were citizens but were not allowed to vote. Slaves, minors [those under 18], and foreigners living and working in Athens did not have citizenship rights.) Aristotle also wrote that the best life is lived by those who try to live lives of virtue. This means that if a person always tries to do the right thing, even when it is difficult or uncomfortable, he will live his life in the best way.

Aristotle wrote that there is something "just by nature." This means that justice cannot mean one thing in one society and another thing in another society, because there is a higher law than the one created by man. This idea can be called nature's law, or natural law. Aristotle also wrote that happiness is "activity of soul in accordance with nature," meaning a life lived in accordance with reason and virtue is a happy one.

Although ancient Greece flourished over 2,000 years ago, Americans believe and think in many ways similar to the ancient Greeks. The Founding Fathers who started the United States of America saw ancient Greeks and Romans as our ancestors and they even built many buildings in our nation's capital city to resemble those of ancient Greece and Rome. Our U.S. Capitol (where our Congressmen work), the Supreme Court building (where our most important judges work), and the White House were all built in the Neoclassical architectural style to resemble those found in ancient Greece and Rome.

Chapter 3

THE ROMAN REPUBLIC

Another great pillar for Western Civilization is the Roman Republic (509 B.C. to 48 B.C.). The American Founding Fathers looked closely at the Roman Republic when writing our governing document, the Constitution. The philosophy of the Romans greatly influenced Americans. In addition, America's most beloved leader, George Washington, was and still is compared to one of Rome's greatest generals and farmers, Cincinnatus.

Romans tried to create a government in which its citizens were treated the same by the law, and where a strong man could not become the dictator. In the Roman Republic, citizens were adult, free males who lived within the Roman Republic and who were not from a colony or province. Before and after the Roman Republic, the world is full of examples of determined, brutal leaders who took over and ruled a government by force, yet in the Roman Republic, each citizen could vote, and the powers of government were separated into three branches, just like in the Greek and American governments.

All Romans had to follow the law. This idea is known as "the rule of law." It is important, because in most countries of the world then, and in many today, leaders do not have to follow the law and can change it as they like. So, if one day a leader wants to steal someone's jewels, he can, and if a poor person gets things taken from him, there is nothing he can do about it. In Rome, however, the laws, called the Twelve Tables, were publicly displayed, every citizen was under the law, and children memorized the laws. When laws are written, society is secure because everyone knows what is allowed or not allowed. The powerful cannot assert their will over others if it means breaking the legal code.

Romans also believed in freedom of thought, freedom of speech, that a person was innocent until proven guilty, and that the accused has a right to confront his accuser. All of these ideas are important in American society today. Freedom of thought means that each person has a right to think, even if his thoughts may offend others. Freedom of speech means that a person can say what he thinks, even if he opposes the government. When we say the accused has a right to confront his accuser and that a person is innocent until proven guilty, it means that a person accused of a crime has the right to see the person who accused him, and the accuser must present evidence to show guilt.

Cincinnatus was a 5th century Roman who wanted to farm his land. However, enemy tribes were attacking Rome and his fellow countrymen needed his military leadership. They made him dictator so that he could defend Rome, and give orders to everyone quickly and decisively. However, two weeks after the Romans defeated their enemies, Cincinnatus peacefully gave up his power and went back to being a farmer. Romans and historians honor Cincinnatus as an example of a great and humble leader. Many years later, after leading the Continental Army during the American Revolution, George Washington also stepped down from power, and he surrendered power again when he resigned after his second presidential term. Many historians say that Washington acted just like Cincinnatus, displaying courage in the same way.

Cicero (106 B.C. to 43 B.C.) was a Roman statesman who wrote about man and his rights. The American Founding Fathers read his works, which greatly influenced them. Cicero wrote that true law is based on reason and that it is the same for all men everywhere in the world. Like Aristotle, he wrote that all men everywhere are ruled by something called natural law that humans have because of their birth. No great person or leader gives this natural law to someone. We have it because we are born.

Cicero strongly believed in the idea of representative government, and eventually gave up his life for it. Representative government is a system where citizens vote for their leaders, and their leaders rule with the idea of doing what is best for the citizens. When citizens grow unhappy with their leaders, they can vote the leaders out. This system is called republicanism. At the end of the Roman Republic, Cicero wrote strongly opposing Romans Octavian, Lepidus, and Antony, who wanted a dictatorship. As a result, they proclaimed Cicero an enemy of the state, killed him, and the tyrannical Roman Empire replaced the Roman Republic.

CHRISTIANITY

During the first century, a new religion began that would eventually become the official religion of the Roman Empire and spread throughout the Western world. Jesus Christ was a Jewish carpenter born and raised in Roman-controlled Bethlehem and Nazareth in the ancient Near East. His followers, called Christians, taught that Jesus was the son of God, that he was a savior to all people, and that all people are called to turn from their selfish ways, ask God for forgiveness, and treat each other with love. Three centuries after the death of Christ, Christians compiled this message in the Bible, their holy book. The Bible, in Romans 1:19, 2:14-15 (English Standard Version), states:

> *For what can be known about God is plain to them, because God has shown it to them...When gentiles [non-Christians] who have not the law do by nature what the law requires, they are a law to themselves, even though they do not have the law. They show that what the law requires is written in their hearts, while their conscience also bears witness...*

Christians believe that all people were created in the image of God, and that all people share the same nature. According to Christians, people know what is good or bad because God gave a conscience to all people. This law of nature exists outside of man's creation. Christians believed this idea over the centuries, and it found expression in the Declaration of Independence, when Thomas Jefferson wrote "all men are created equal" by their Creator.

The development of Christianity within the Roman Empire had ramifications not only for the empire, but for all of Western Civilization. The leader of the Roman Empire, the emperor, led the official Roman religion, which was pagan. The emperor took the title of Pontifex Maximus, meaning leader of the official pagan religion of Rome. When the Roman Empire adopted Christianity in A.D. 380, however, the emperors ceased being head of the religion. This fell to the bishop of Rome, who was called the Pope, forming a separation between the leader of the political world (the emperor) and the religious world (the Pope). Whereas the emperor formerly held ultimate authority in both the political and religious worlds, he was now limited by the Christian Church.

Governments in Western Civilization have expressed the understanding that the political world should be governed by someone different than the leader of the religious world. In North America, this idea can be seen in the constitutions of the English colonies, and in the United States Constitution, notably in the First Amendment. Americans may worship freely in any religion they choose, and they do not have to belong to a particular religious group. This concept of church and state having separate leaders had its beginnings with the Roman Empire.

President Calvin Coolidge, on the 150th anniversary of the Declaration of Independence, wrote that the individual "is endowed with inalienable rights which no majority, however great, and no power of the Government, however broad, can ever be justified in violating. The principle of equality is recognized. It follows inevitably from belief in the brotherhood of man through the fatherhood of God." The belief that an individual has rights over the power of government is one of the great ideas of Western Civilization.

Chapter 4

Western Civilization

"Western Civilization" defines cultures that draw their ways of living from the ancient Fertile Crescent civilizations, the Greeks, and the Romans, as well as from the religious beliefs of Judaism and Christianity. It is called "Western" because it had its beginnings in Near Asia, in the Fertile Crescent, and in ancient and medieval times this way of living spread west into the European world. Another term that describes the same ideas as "Western Civilization" is "Greco-Roman, Judeo-Christian culture."

Beliefs and Practices of Western Civilization

Western Civilization usually means that a society has the following characteristics:

1. Belief in One God
2. Belief in Morality (a Good and a Bad)
3. Natural Law
4. The Rule of Law
5. Written Law
6. Limited Government
7. Political Liberty of All Citizens
8. Rights of the Accused

The first three beliefs and practices of a Western society are very closely related. Belief in one God means that the people believe that one Creator made everything and established a natural order where there is a good and a bad for all humans, and that humans are born with the potential to do both good and bad. When societies believe in many gods, or no God, it is unclear what is good and bad. Many ancient peoples believed in multiple gods who would contradict each other. There was no definitive idea of right and wrong. Morality and natural law stem from the idea that all humans share a common nature and that there is a natural order in which all humans live, supported

21

by both reason and faith.

The rule of law and written law are important Western concepts. The rule of law means that all citizens have to follow the law, even the leaders. This idea ensures that a strong political figure can never abuse citizens. Writing a law makes it somewhat difficult to change. A leader cannot suddenly change the law to suit his desires, which may hurt other citizens.

The last three ideas related to Western Civilization—limited government, political liberty of all citizens, and rights of the accused—are concepts meant to guarantee individuals the freedom they naturally are born with. When a government becomes too big, it takes away the rights and liberties of individuals. If leaders have the power to do everything for people (clothe them, feed them, house them, etc.), then the people do not have any freedom to decide these important matters for themselves. The more the government does for people, the less liberty people have.

Today, in Western Civilization, people have more freedom and liberty than in other civilizations. The weak are protected against the strong. Women have equal political rights with men. Slavery is outlawed. Prisoners have rights, and those accused of crimes have rights. In many countries that are not considered part of Western Civilization, or "The West," we see the practice of slavery, women who are not allowed to vote or even drive a car, and accused people who have absolutely no rights. Life is much better for all citizens in a Western society.

The United States of America was founded on the ideas of Western Civilization. Americans enjoy many freedoms because we have inherited these ideas and beliefs which value the rights of individuals.

UNIT II

America's Medieval Heritage

Introduction

The events and people of medieval history greatly influenced the foundation and history of the United States of America. From the time the Roman Empire collapsed in A.D. 476 to the discovery of America in 1492, the civilizations that would found the United States went through great changes. Modern America was born from the medieval world.

The founders of the United States of America were primarily Western Europeans, of English and French ancestry, although America could not have been formed without the experiences of other Europeans, Asians, Africans, and American Indians. Europeans played a larger role than other nationalities in the foundation of America, thus historians place greater emphasis on medieval European history in order to understand the heritage of the United States. Medieval Asians, Africans, and American Indians did influence the early United States of America, but not to the extent that the Europeans did.

The Dark Ages in medieval Europe refers to the period between the 5th and 10th centuries. During this time, barbarian Germanic, Slavic, and Celtic societies were transformed. In the 5th century, these peoples were pagan, some practiced human sacrifice, and most were illiterate. These ancient tribes conquered and ruled where the Roman Empire had once dominated. Christian missionaries from the Roman Catholic Church, such as Saint Benedict, Saint Boniface, and Saint Patrick converted the pagan Europeans to Christianity. Because of the actions of the Church, the newly converted European Christians adopted Roman systems of government and law, and began to establish higher institutions of learning. The modern people of Europe were born during the first five centuries of the medieval ages.

From 1000 to 1500, Europeans established complex societies, banking systems, the beginning of capitalism, higher forms of art and literature, and invented and developed a high level of technology in many areas. Europeans rediscovered cultural advances of the ancient world and had a rebirth of interest in classical life during a period called the Renaissance. Adventurers and leaders were excited to discover new lands and to acquire riches. And, in 1492, Catholic Spain completed the Reconquista, or reconquering, taking Spain back from the Muslims who had controlled Spain since the 700s.

In 1492, Europeans, and especially Spaniards, were eager to spread the Christian faith, open up new markets, and explore the world. Spanish King Ferdinand and Queen Isabella agreed to sponsor Genoese explorer Christopher Columbus to seek a faster passage to Asia. Though Columbus believed he found India, instead, he opened up colonization of North and South America to all the European countries. The British established 13 English colonies in America, and these would later become the United States of America.

Throughout the medieval ages in England, the English people incrementally limited the power of the king and of the government. The English thought that the less power the government had, the more liberty the people could enjoy. In 1215, King John was forced to sign the Magna Carta. The Magna Carta limited the power of the monarch and granted rights to noblemen. In 1289, Parliament was formed. Parliament is made up of representatives and it has the power to pass laws. In 1689, Parliament passed the English Bill of Rights, which guaranteed liberties to English citizens. When the Americans established their republic, they drew from hundreds of years of an English government that was limited in power. Because of medieval history, when Americans formed the United States of America, their intent was to create a government that had as few powers as necessary in order to guarantee rights to the individuals.

Chapter 5

The Age of Barbarians

The Age of Barbarians marks roughly the first 400 to 500 years of the medieval ages, from A.D. 476 to about 900 or 1000. Sometimes called "The Dark Ages," it was a time of violence, great uncertainty, and chaos throughout Europe and the former Western Roman Empire. As the Roman Empire crumbled, the Germanic, Slavic, and Hun peoples stepped in to take over. Although the barbarian tribesmen lacked the education, sophistication, and culture of the Romans, the barbarians eventually destroyed the Roman Empire and ruled Europe for centuries.

When Romans travelled into northern Europe, they came into contact with Germanic tribesmen, a people with a different culture and language than the Romans. One Roman author remarked that when he heard the Germanic peoples speaking, he could only hear the sounds of "bar bar bar bar." Because of this, Romans called people who spoke another language than Latin, as well as those who seemed uncultured, barbarians. The Germanic barbarians had no written language, a simpler political organization than the Romans, and worshipped trees and nature. Romans came to look at all of the people outside of its northern borders as barbarians, even though there were differences among the various groups.

The Germanic peoples were not the only ones migrating west and south and destroying Roman culture. From Asia came the Huns, warriors on horseback who invaded the peoples of Europe in the fifth century. Attila was chief of the Huns and one of the most feared conquerors in history. After laying waste to much of Italy and Rome in A.D. 452, Attila had plans to destroy the Vatican City in Rome. However, Pope Leo the Great rode out of Rome with his entourage and engaged Attila in discussion. No one knows what was said during this conversation, but Attila did not attack the Vatican City, leaving the early Christian Church intact.

Celtic and Slavic peoples also inhabited Europe. Like the Germanic tribes and Huns, they lacked a written language and were polytheists (believed in many gods). Celts were known as fierce warriors with a great sense of political equality. Celtic women could speak and vote in tribal councils and could carry weapons and fight in battle. Celtic peoples inhabited Central and Western Europe. Slavic peoples inhabited Central and Eastern Europe. It is believed Vikings (from Denmark, Norway, and Sweden) enslaved large numbers of Slavs, from which our English word "slave" originated.

The Germanic, Hun, Celtic, and Slavic peoples all shared many characteristics that greatly contrasted with the Romans of the fifth century. The barbarians were polytheists; the Romans Christians. Some of the barbarians practiced human sacrifice; the Romans thought this practice horrifying. The barbarians lacked reading and writing; the Romans valued learning. In all societies, slavery was the norm. Contrary to popular belief, there is no evidence that Romans used toilet paper and barbarians did not. It appears that neither society used paper.

Throughout the old and crumbling Roman Empire, various barbarian tribes conquered and settled: the Angles, Saxons, and Jutes in Britain; the Franks and Burgundians in modern-day France; the Visigoths and Vandals in modern-day Spain and North Africa; the Ostrogoths in modern-day Italy; the Slavs in Central Europe; the Celts in modern-day Ireland, Scotland, and Wales. These peoples would eventually form the modern nations of Europe.

CHAPTER 6

CIVILIZING EUROPE

From the end of the Roman Empire (A.D. 476) to about the year 1000, one of the greatest and most rapid changes in history occurred. The various tribes of Europe went from being illiterate to literate, from living as tribes to living in organized kingdoms, from living as people ruled only by physical might to citizens living under the law. Chaos and violence gave way to order and peace. By 1000, for the average person in Europe, life, though not perfect, was much better than it had been.

One institution survived the fall of the Roman Empire—the Christian Church, centered in Rome, with the Pope as its head. Christians trace the beginning of their Church to Jesus choosing the Apostle Peter as the first leader of the Church. In the first century, Church Fathers called this the Church universal, because it was the first religion in the world that was open to all people of all nations. Universal translates from Greek into the word "Catholic." This is why the early Christians called themselves Catholic.

Early Christians were fervent missionaries who wanted to spread the message of Christianity throughout the world. In medieval times, the chief missionaries to the pagan Germanic, Celtic, and Slavic tribes of Europe were monks. Monks were Christian men who devoted their lives to God and the Church, took vows of celibacy, spent their time working among the poor, teaching better methods of agriculture, and persuading pagan peoples to give up their faith and sometimes horrific practices, such as sacrificing humans. Monks ran hospitals and also preserved and promoted the best literature of the world by copying Latin script and teaching others.

Great missionaries went out to the pagan peoples and began the drastic change in the medieval world. St. Patrick (c. 387-493) was a Britain who had been imprisoned in Ireland by Celtic pirates. He escaped and returned to

Ireland as a bishop and is attributed with converting the whole country. The Catholic Church still sends Irish priests throughout the world as missionaries. St. Benedict of Nursia (480-547) was the first to establish monasteries, thus setting up the system that would play an integral role in changing Europe. St. Boniface (c. 675-754), a missionary to the Germanic peoples, was killed by someone who rejected his missionary work. St. Cyril and St. Methodius, ninth century missionaries to the Slavic people, began the conversion of the Russians, Poles, Czechs, and Southern Slavs.

In addition to Christianity, Europeans saw the advantages of the Roman way of life in political, economic and cultural areas, and thus adopted Roman practices. Leaders in each nation learned how to read and write Latin, developed their own written language, created common legal systems, and established kingdoms that became the modern countries of Europe.

CHAPTER 7

FOUNDATION OF EUROPEAN KINGDOMS

The modern nations of Europe trace their foundations to their medieval kingdoms. In every kingdom, Christianity played a key role in the foundation period. The Franks founded the first European kingdom in the fifth century. This later became the kingdoms of the French, the Germans, and the Italians. The kingdom of England was founded in the ninth century, followed by the Russian kingdom in the tenth and eleventh centuries. By 1200, all of the major European kingdoms had been founded, and the foundation for modern Europe had been set.

The Franks, a Germanic tribe occupying the area around modern-day Paris, France, began their kingdom in the fifth century. Clovis I converted to the faith of his wife, Catholic Christianity, and brought his nation into the same church. Clovis began the Merovingian Dynasty, which would lead the Frankish Empire for two centuries. (A dynasty is a ruling family.)

The next dynasty that ruled the Franks was the Carolingian. In 732, Charles Martel (Charles the Hammer) would lead the Franks in defeating the Muslim invaders of Europe, saving the continent from conversion to Islam. His grandson, Charlemagne (Charles the Great), united much of central Europe, forcefully converting many of the European tribes. Charlemagne was crowned Holy Roman Emperor and tried to bring back the glory of Rome united with the Christian faith. Charlemagne encouraged learning in his empire and enforced strict adherence to Christianity throughout his realm. Charlemagne's three grandchildren became leaders of kingdoms that would eventually become France, Germany, and Italy.

King Alfred the Great founded the medieval kingdom of England by the ninth century. Alfred, the only English king called great, united the Angles and Saxons, established a Christian kingdom, defeated the pagan Vikings, and encouraged learning. Today, Queen Elizabeth II is a direct descendent of Alfred! For over 1,000 years one family has been English royalty.

Medieval Russia had been strongly influenced by Slavic and Viking pagan beliefs and practices until St. Vladimir I converted to Christianity around A.D. 1000. Prince Vladimir had lived a common pagan life, had many wives, and had erected shrines to Viking and Slavic gods. He then converted to Christianity, chose one wife, and converted so many Russians that he is called "Apostle of the Russians." He firmly established the Eastern Orthodox Christian Church (religion of the Eastern Roman Empire, also called Byzantium) in Russia.

Chapter 8

Development of Liberty in Medieval England

Throughout nearly the entire medieval world, governments had almost absolute power over the lives of the people they governed. The role of the subject was to serve the lord and king. The nobility had more rights than everyone else. Only a medieval lord could own land, for example. To go against one's lord or the king meant to go against God. Nevertheless, the principles of liberty and limited government developed in medieval England. Combined with ancient precedents, these principles later inspired the American Founding Fathers to create the first modern republic where citizens would enjoy more rights than anywhere else in the world.

For centuries, families from Anglo-Saxon or Danish peoples ruled England. In 1066, William of Normandy invaded England and made himself king, establishing a feudal order that had already existed in all of Europe. The feudal order was based on the idea of exchanging land for loyalty and the idea that each person had obligations to the local lord and community. Each member of society had a role to fulfill, and the leaders of the feudal order had more rights than anyone else. After 1066, King William and the Normans ruled England.

Over the following centuries, the English established practices and laws that whittled away the power of the kings and the nobility to rule without question. In the early 1200s, one of England's least popular kings, King John, tried to raise taxes on the lords and burghers (townsmen). Because King John was unpopular and had waged some unsuccessful wars, the lords rebelled against him. Instead of handing more tax money to King John, in 1215 the lords forced the king to sign a document, called the Magna Carta, which limited his power.

The Magna Carta
1. Stated that if the king wanted to raise taxes, he had to ask permission of the lords and burghers.
2. Gave nobles and burghers the right to "due process of law." Due process of law means:
   A. If the king were to punish someone, the king had to show by legal means what wrong the person had committed.
   B. The principle of trial by jury, that an accused person is guaranteed a trial with a group of people who would determine his innocence or guilt.
   C. Habeas corpus, the idea that the government cannot lock someone in jail without a valid reason.

Medieval English judges established the principle of common law. A common law meant that all of England would follow the same law, instead of having local laws that varied in nature. This common law was not found in one written document, but in the oral traditions and decisions of English court cases. Common law established the idea that English law could not change at the whim of the leader. Common law is unwritten, passed on by judges in oral tradition.

In 1289, King Edward I assembled a group of nobles with the intention of having them vote for higher taxes to support a war. However, this initial meeting developed into the English Parliament, which became the body of men who create the law in England. Parliament has two houses, an upper house (House of Lords) which consists of church leaders and nobles, and a lower house (House of Commons) which consists of knights and local citizen leaders. Members of the House of Commons are non-aristocratic burghers and townspeople.

When the American Founding Fathers formed the United States of America, they knew of the centuries of English experience in limiting the power of the government, starting in the medieval ages. The country that they formed benefitted from the liberties that the English had won from the kings.

CONSTITUTIONALISM

Constitutionalism is a set of ideas, attitudes, and behaviors based on the principle that the authority of government comes from a body of fundamental law. It means that government is limited by its laws and the practices of law and government over a period of time. A related concept, the rule of law, means that laws govern a country, not the opinions and whims of its rulers. Constitutionalism and the rule of law are two concepts that make it impossible for a ruler to take full control of a government.

In Great Britain, constitutionalism developed in the Middle Ages and was accepted by British citizens as the best principle to limit the power of rulers. When Englishmen later colonized North America, they wrote principles of constitutionalism into the governments of the colonies. When the American Founding Fathers created the U.S. Constitution, they put in writing nearly all the constitutional concepts the English had believed in for centuries.

Chapter 9

The Crusades

In 1095, Pope Urban II called for a massive religious war. The Crusades were a series of wars that Christian Europeans waged against Muslim Turks to free the Holy Land from Islamic control. They became a culture-changing event that opened up the rest of the world to the Europeans, leading to the growth of business, the Renaissance, and the discovery of America. Within four centuries after the Crusades, the medieval ages ended, and Columbus' great discovery of America began the colonization of the New World. A part of this New World would become the United States of America.

Islam is a religion founded by Muhammad, a seventh century Arab. Followers of Islam, called Muslims, believe in one God to whom all must submit. Medieval Muslims believed that they were called by God to conquer and convert the world.

For over 1,000 years, the Holy Land, the area of greatest religious importance for Jews and Christians, was controlled by the Greeks and then the Romans. In the 600s, the Islamic Caliphate of the Arabs captured Jerusalem and the Holy Land from the Orthodox Christian Eastern Roman Empire (also known as Byzantium). In the early years of Islamic rule, the Arab Muslims allowed Christian pilgrims to travel safely to the Holy Land. Turkish Muslims then conquered the land, and did not allow Christian pilgrims safe travel. The Turks threatened Constantinople, the capital city of Byzantium, and wanted to eventually conquer all of Europe. Because of these events, Pope Urban II called for a Crusade to free the Holy Land from the Muslims and stop the threat to the rest of Europe.

The Crusaders failed to take and maintain control of the Holy Land, but they forced the Muslim leaders to allow Christian pilgrims to visit. Perhaps more importantly, Crusaders witnessed the beauty and splendor of Asia, tried Asian spices that made food taste much better, and brought home beautifully colored textiles that Europeans had never seen. Europeans became eager to establish trade with the East and bring the best of Asia to their homes.

As a result, trade between Asia and Europe grew, European coastal cities such as Florence, Italy, became wealthy, and the growing merchant class in Europe benefitted from the exchange. However, to obtain the riches from Asia, European merchants had to pay Arab and Asian middle men who traveled along the Silk Road from Far East Asia to the Mediterranean Sea. The Silk Road was the path traders took, bringing silk, spices, and textiles from China to the Near East and then into Europe. Europeans wanted a quicker and less expensive route to Asia. Thus the exploration age of Europe was born, in part, out of the European desire to seek a quicker trade route to Asia.

Chapter 10

The Age of Exploration and Christopher Columbus

In the 1400s, Western Europeans rapidly modernized, experienced a social mobility never before imaginable, developed high forms of art, and used technology in new ways. The Renaissance that started in Italian city-states spread north, and throughout Europe there was a sense that the world waited to be explored, discovered, conquered and civilized by those who were brave and eager enough. Europeans were eager to spread the Catholic Christian faith to all corners of the world. During the Renaissance, European artists and intellectuals rediscovered the beauty and knowledge of the ancient Greek and Roman artists and intellectuals. City-states in Italy grew wealthy from trade with the East through the Mediterranean Sea, and countries in Western Europe wanted to go directly to the East by ocean, without having to go through the Mediterranean Sea and dealing with middle men.

Before Columbus discovered America, Spanish and Portuguese sailors led the exploration of the world. The sailors' original goal was to reach India and the Far East by going around Africa. Although today we can see how to go around the south of Africa, people of the 1400s did not know how big Africa was, and traveling into unknown places without any maps is always terrifying.

In Portugal, the son of the king built a home overlooking the ocean and formed a school where sailors learned how to read maps and sail the ocean, all with the goal of sailing around the southern part of Africa to go to Asia. Because of his dedication and accomplishments, he is called Prince Henry the Navigator. Prince Henry died in 1463, before any of his sailors had succeeded in rounding the southern tip of Africa. Still, his ideas and school caught the imagination of sailors around the world.

Within 34 years after the death of Prince Henry, not only did Portuguese sailors sail around the southern tip of Africa, but they navigated to India and changed the center of trading power from the Turks on the Mediterranean to the Western Europeans on the Atlantic. In 1486, Portuguese explorer Bartholomew Diaz succeeded in sailing around the southern tip of Africa. In 1497, Vasco de Gama sailed to India and back to Portugal, bringing caskets of jewels, rich spices packaged in silk, and incredible textiles. Portugal became the strongest sea power in the world.

Throughout the 1500s to the 1800s, the European countries of Holland, Great Britain, and France joined Spain and Portugal in exploring the world. The Spanish explored South America and the southern part of North America, establishing a huge empire and spreading the Catholic faith among native peoples. Holland, Great Britain, and France explored and established colonies in North America that would eventually become the United States of America and Canada. Although all of these explorations are important, Christopher Columbus stands out in the minds and hearts of modern Americans, because he has grown to become a main point of debate about European exploration and the native population of the Americas.

CHRISTOPHER COLUMBUS

There are those who will argue, "Christopher Columbus really did not discover America. There were people there already. The Indians were there." And there are those who will say, "The Vikings travelled to North America centuries before Columbus. Leif Ericson the Norsemen discovered America." But these people really do not understand the meaning behind the phrase, "Columbus discovered America." Of course, the Native Americans inhabited both North and South America before Columbus and the Spanish came, and Leif Ericson did establish a colony in North America in the medieval ages.

However, none of the pre-Columbian discoveries had any impact on the rest of the world. The American Indians did not know of the continents they lived on, and they could not communicate this reality to the rest of the world because they lacked a written language and the technology and desire to go to other continents. The Norsemen's colony disappeared, and we did not learn of it until after the new land had been settled. Columbus' great discovery had a monumental impact on the history of the world. His finding a route to America opened up two new continents to the world, and opened up the world to the Native Americans. To deny or belittle this is to deny reality.

Christopher Columbus (1451-1506) was an explorer, cartographer (map maker), and adventurer from the Republic of Genoa (today part of northern Italy). In 1492, he led an expedition from Spain and discovered the islands of the West Indies. He died believing he had found a westerly route to Asia, but in reality he had opened up the continents of North America and South America for European discovery and colonization. Fifty years ago, Americans viewed Columbus as a hero, and schoolchildren across the country had Columbus Day off from school. Today, students in only a few states honor Columbus, and people in many parts of our country view him with great dislike. Columbus Day is celebrated in some places of the United States on the second Monday of October, sometimes falling on the day he discovered America, October 12, 1492.

Beginning in 711, Spain was ruled by a foreign power called the Moors. The Moors were Muslim conquerors from Africa and had tried to convert all of Spain to Islam, imposing a special tax on non-Muslims and treating non-Muslims as second class citizens. From the very beginning of Muslim rule, the Spanish had waged a war against the Moors, called the "Reconquista." In 1492, the Spanish defeated the last Muslim army, and after this 700-year war, Spain was filled with unbounded confidence and believed it was a chosen country to explore, Christianize, and conquer the world. King Ferdinand and Queen Isabella of Spain, fresh from their victory over the Muslims, agreed to allow the explorer Christopher Columbus to use Spanish ships and men to go on his quest. Columbus set out in three ships: the Niña, the Pinta, and the Santa Maria. His goals were to find a new trade route to Asia, to find gold and bring it back to Spain, to map and explore the land he reached, to claim new land for Spain, and to spread Catholic Christianity throughout the world. Columbus believed that by sailing west from Spain, he would eventually arrive in India. After approximately 30 days, Columbus found a new land. However, as we know, it was not Asia; it was an island in the Bahamas. Columbus believed he had found India and called the natives "Indians."

Columbus made four separate journeys to the Bahamas and established Spanish forts, though he could not find gold, and was even arrested by the Spanish for being an incompetent and tyrannical governor of the new lands. Columbus' men were so intent on finding gold that they mistreated many of the Indians they encountered. Historical accounts document torture and murder by some of Columbus' men. Columbus was either unable or unwilling to stop them. The Spanish king and queen arrested Columbus, had him brought him back to Spain in chains, tried him for incompetence and for the cruel treatment some of his men perpetrated against the Indians, and jailed him. Yet in six weeks, the king released him.

Columbus' legacy in the New World is mixed. He discovered America and opened up new lands for the rest of the world. Before Columbus, Indians in the Americas worshipped multiple gods, many practiced torture and polygamy, and some practiced cannibalism as a way of life. Europeans who came and settled the Americas brought monotheism and ended polygamy. Eventually, they established the United States of America and all other countries of North and South America. Columbus' discovery of America led to the founding of these modern nations. Columbus has also been the focus of those who argue that the European conquest of the Americas was an immoral act against the Indians. The group of Indians Columbus first encountered, the Tainos, were extinct 50 years later. Most Indians who came into contact with the Spanish and other Europeans died from new diseases, such as smallpox. The natives had no immunity built up against these illnesses. European disease is believed to have killed up to 90% of the Indian population. And, the superior military strength of the Europeans made it easier to destroy the Indian culture.

Many negative beliefs about Christopher Columbus and the Spanish who commissioned his explorations are historically false. Historians called revisionists have created a false history, or they have under-reported (not reported everything), in order to paint an untrue picture of Columbus and Spain. Authors Michael Allen and Larry Schweikart make the following points about this false history:

1. Revisionist historians say Columbus committed "genocide" against the Indians, but genocide means a deliberate attempt to kill a whole people. Columbus and his men never had a goal to kill all the Indians. In fact, Columbus was arrested for poorly controlling his soldiers. Most Indians who died due to European contact died because of diseases such as smallpox. Neither the Spanish nor the Indians knew how diseases were transmitted, and there were no vaccines available at the time.

2. Revisionists claim native populations of up to 60 million, but more reasonable estimates range from 1.8 million to 8 million. Historians do not argue with the fact that European diseases killed up to 90% of Indians, however, revisionist historians have exaggerated the numbers of Indians killed to make it appear that the tragedy was worse and to claim genocide. However, the Spanish had no policy of exterminating Indians. In fact, the Spanish wanted to include the Indians in the Spanish Empire.

3. Some diseases spread through native populations before Europeans arrived. Some Indians died of disease before the arrival of Europeans.

4. Native populations engaged in balance of power tactics similar to those used by European countries during the 1900s, and many constantly battled with each other before Columbus arrived. The Aztecs controlled the area of present-day Mexico City, and ruled their neighboring tribes with unbelievable ferocity. A conservative estimate numbers annual Aztec human sacrifices in the thousands. When Spanish soldiers came to conquer the Aztecs, many Aztec enemies volunteered to fight with the Spanish.

Before the 1960s, American students and historians focused on the positive elements of Columbus' discovery of America, and all America celebrated him. In 1971, Columbus Day became a federal holiday. After this, however, certain states began to cancel the celebration of Columbus. In California, for example, students do not celebrate Columbus Day. On the other hand, New Yorkers, especially Italian Americans, herald Columbus as a hero. New York City has a huge Columbus Day parade with over 35,000 people every year. Unfortunately, many American students today do not know anything about Christopher Columbus.

CHAPTER 11

THE REFORMATION AND THE ENLIGHTENMENT

THE REFORMATION

In 1529, German Catholic priest Martin Luther began a separation that arguably became the most important in Christianity, and this act had great impact on the United States of America hundreds of years later. Martin Luther became upset with the one Christian Church in Europe, the Roman Catholic Church. He thought that the Catholic Church abused its power, kept average people from knowing God, and did not understand how people were saved. Luther argued that each person should read the Bible in his or her own language and that the Pope was not the earthly representative of Christ. Many German princes agreed with Luther and helped him form the Lutheran Church. Followers of Luther were called Protestants, because they protested the teachings and actions of the Catholic Church. Over the next 150 years, many other Protestant churches formed, including the Anglican Church in England. In Europe, people fought each other over religious differences. In America, the great majority of settlers were Protestants, and they very often split from their own churches to form new Protestant religious groups.

Protestant beliefs and ideas about government, religion, and hard work had a large impact on the founding of America. Protestants tended to not trust in an all-powerful government, and constantly tried to limit the power of the king. Protestants hold that a person reaches salvation through faith, not by works. However, the ones who settled America also believed that God showered blessings on those who worked hard. This became known as the Protestant work ethic. Protestants also believed in the necessity of reading and understanding the Bible. In America, this meant that the great majority of Americans learned how to read.

Religious freedom was born in America. During the first 150 years of colonization in America, most colonies had official religions and did not allow anyone to practice another religion. However, a few colonies had freedom of religion from their founding, namely Rhode Island, Pennsylvania, and Maryland. By the time of the American Revolution, all Americans had freedom of religion.

The Enlightenment

In many ways, the United States of America is a child of the Enlightenment, a European intellectual movement of the late 17th and 18th centuries which emphasized reason and individualism rather than tradition. This movement was heavily influenced by 17th-century philosophers such as Descartes, Locke, Newton, Goethe, Voltaire, Smith, and Rousseau, as well as 18th-century philosopher Kant.

Enlightenment thinkers, predominantly strong Christians, believed that following the philosophies of reason and individualism enabled humans to live and organize governments in the best way. Englishman John Locke wrote about political freedom, and how every person was created by God with the right to life, liberty, and private property. English writer Adam Smith wrote that individuals should be allowed to choose what to create, what to buy, and how to make financial decisions free from governmental control. Smith's writings form the basis for the 18th- and 19th-century understanding of capitalism. Thinkers of the Enlightenment greatly influenced the American Founding Fathers, who then implemented Enlightenment philosophy into the American system of government and economics.

UNIT III

European Colonization of America

Introduction

When Europeans explored and colonized North and South America, they did not come to a completely empty land. Native Americans, who Columbus called Indians, lived there. There were approximately 1.8 million to 8 million Indians when Columbus set foot in America. Within a few hundred years, the Indian way of life would give way to European culture, and Indian civilization would be almost completely lost.

According to historians, European civilization was able to replace Indian culture due to many reasons. First of all, as Michael Allen and Larry Schweikart write, Christians believed "there was a rational God capable of being known through reason as well as faith." Nearly all Europeans were Christians, and strived to find the truth in reason. This caused the Europeans to question things, to want to advance in knowledge of their world, and to develop technology. Secondly, Europeans coupled that technological inquisitiveness with political and economic risk-taking. This means that Europeans wanted to develop better tools to improve their lives, even at the risk of what they had. Thirdly, the English developed a business model that allowed for individuals to invest their money along with others into a joint-stock company in order to make a profit. This allowed for large projects led by a group of individuals seeking personal gain, such as the founding of America's first colony, Jamestown. Lastly, Europeans promoted literacy, which allows people to learn from previous generations. The American Indians had none of these elements in their culture, and thus were at a great disadvantage to the Europeans.

CHAPTER 12
NATIVE AMERICANS

Native Americans, or Indians, lived throughout North and South America when European explorers and settlers came into contact with them. In terms of technology, most Indians had primitive societies. The Indians who lived in what became the United States of America lacked a written language, used Stone Age tools because they lacked knowledge to form metal into productive uses, were similar to pre-Hebraic cultures in that they were polytheistic (believed in many gods), and had minimal protections against disease and wild animals. Most Indians practiced slavery, and a man could have as many wives as he could feed through his hunting. Commonly, a victorious Indian tribe captured all women in a defeated tribe and forced them to become wives. One interesting fact about the people we call Native Americans, or Indians, is that even their ancestors migrated to the Americas. So, like all other people in the United States, Indians can trace their ancestry to other continents.

A few problems Americans have in understanding Indians involve the great variety of different Indian societies, the power of inaccurate modern movies, and the desire of many Americans to show that every aspect of every other culture is good. Some of the Indian tribes were extremely peaceful, and others were warlike. Most Indians did not live in tipis and hunt buffalo with horses, and those who did hunt buffalo did not always use every part of every animal they hunted. When the Plains Indians needed buffalo meat to eat, they would kill a buffalo and leave the hide. When they needed the hide to make tipis, they would kill buffalo for their hides and leave the flesh to rot. When the Northeast Indians would use up the area in which they lived in their villages, they would leave their structures and human waste and simply move to unused territory. One cannot really say that this is respecting nature; rather, it is merely using the best that nature has to offer.

Geography and climate greatly influenced Indians because of their lack of technology. They lived in either agricultural, nomadic, hunting, or fishing tribal societies. There were over 300 tribes, each with its own language and customs, within the area of the present-day United States of America. In this area, anthropologists identify three cultural groups: Woodland (East of the Mississippi River), Plains, and Coastal (West Coast) Indians. Woodland Indians were agricultural, and Plains and Coastal Indians were hunters and gatherers.

American Indians, a religious people, made rituals an important part of their lives. One practice of some Plains Indians, called the Sun Dance, involved a ritual where Indian men went through a physically painful act, seeking spiritual gifts or powers. Those who had pledged to do the Sun Dance would dance for many days, without eating or drinking. Then, a ritual leader would pierce the participant's skin on the upper chest or back. Leather straps were laced through the skin, and these were fastened to a pole or to an object. The participant then either hung on the hooks or dragged the object around with the hooks, until the skin broke. Lack of an Indian written language where this practice took place has hindered our understanding of this ritual, but historians believe that when the Indian suffered greatly, he would receive a vision that would help him understand his life.

Woodland Indians were the first that early settlers of America confronted. Male Indians were farmers, hunters, and fishermen, and they made war and gambled, while the Indian women did all of the gathering of fruits, nuts, and roots, the cooking, the raising of the children, and were in charge of the home. Indians, in constant conflict with other tribes, engaged in unwritten treaties for protection. When the European settlers came, Indians viewed them as another Indian tribe, with some tribes becoming allies of the Europeans, and other tribes attempting to destroy them. Woodland Indians fished from the shores of the Great Lakes to the Atlantic Coast. The largest of these tribes formed the Iroquois League, a loose confederation where the tribes agreed to come to each other's defense if one were attacked. Tribes of the Woodlands practiced balance of power politics, allying with other tribes to guarantee their survival.

Other Indians of North America included Plains, Coastal, Southwest, and Arctic. Indians of the Arctic were fishermen and lived in underground houses or igloos on the Pacific or Arctic coasts. Subarctic Indians gathered plants, fished, trapped animals, and hunted mostly caribou. California Indians, fisherman, hunters and gatherers, lived in either small huts or wooden homes. Northwest Coastal Indians were fishermen who lived in wooden houses. Southwest tribes such as the Navajo were an exception to the rule: even though they were close to the Plains, they were farmers of beans and corn and lived in homes made of adobe. Plains Indians initially hunted buffalo on foot. Starting in 1492, Columbus and the Spanish introduced horses to America. Some escaped and were captured by the Plains Indians, who then used these animals to hunt.

Chapter 13

Spanish and French Colonies in America

New Spain

Because of Christopher Columbus, Spain was the first country to take advantage of the possibilities in the new land. Throughout the 1500s, 1600s, and 1700s, Spain sent explorers, colonizers, and Catholic missionaries to the Americas. They established Spain as the greatest presence in the New World before England would even begin to expand. However, the Spanish colonists lacked the freedom and opportunities of the English colonists, and the Spanish colonies in North America would never become as successful as the English colonies. The Spanish Empire was gigantic, but Spain's importance in what became the United States of America was limited. The Spanish Empire in North America encompassed the Southwest, Florida, Texas, and all of Mexico and Central America.

On August 28, 1565, Spanish explorers sighted land while off the coast of present-day Florida. Because the sailors of Spain were Catholic, they founded a city on this land and named it after the saint day of August 28, Saint Augustine. They built a fort, and had a meal of thanksgiving to God, the first thanksgiving meal in North America, though not the most famous and most important one.

The Spanish had been incredibly successful in finding gold among the Aztecs in Mexico and the Incas in South America in the 1500s, and they thought that gold had to be further north as well. To find this gold, Hernando de Soto explored the Southeast and discovered the Mississippi River. Francisco Coronado went in search of the fabled "Seven Cities" of gold in the Southwest, but instead discovered the Grand Canyon. The failure of the Spanish to find gold led them to focus their efforts on colonizing what would become Mexico and South America.

Many Spanish came to America not for gold, but to spread Christianity among the Indians. Spanish missionaries established missions, learned Indian languages that had never before been written down, and in some cases, were tortured and killed by the Indians. Bartolome de Las Casas came to America initially to get rich in the 1500s, but he gave up this desire and became a Catholic priest. For over 50 years, he defended the rights of the Indians, successfully arguing against using Indians as slaves. Also in the 1500s, Father Luis de Cancer went to Florida to convert the Indians, though they rejected his message and scalped him. (To scalp someone means to chop off a chunk of the back of the skull, killing the person.) In the 1700s, Father Junipero Serra established the California missions, a string of 21 settlements that served as churches, hospitals, and centers of agriculture and industry.

New France

Even though Christopher Columbus failed to find a westerly route to Asia, Europeans still believed that there was an all-water route to Asia and searched for a pathway through North America. This path that really did not exist was called the Northwest Passage. French explorer Jacques Cartier tried to find the Northwest Passage, and in the process discovered a large gulf and river he named the St. Lawrence Gulf and the St. Lawrence River. He also found two Indian villages—one later became Quebec and the other he named Montreal, which means Royal Mountain. Though Cartier thought his journeys had been a failure, France laid claim to the land he discovered and established the French Empire in North America. The French Empire would also lay claim to a large area in the center of what would become the United States of America.

In 1608, Samuel de Champlain founded the city of Quebec, located on the banks of the St. Lawrence River in an area perfect for a fort, atop a steep cliff. Champlain wanted to spread Catholicism among the Indians and establish a fur trading settlement that would bring him and France riches. Champlain succeeded in making friends with the Algonquin and Huron Indians, but this brought hatred towards New France from the Iroquois Indians who lived in New York and hated the Algonquin Indians. The Iroquois became friends with the English, and thus the French-English rivalry in North America began right at the founding of the new colonies. Because Champlain founded the first successful French settlement in North America, he is called the Father of New France.

Along with setting up fur trading outposts throughout what would become Canada, the French sent missionaries to the Indians to teach them about Jesus Christ. Father Isaac Jogues left Quebec and travelled over 900 miles by canoe and on foot to the Mohawk Indians. On the journey, the Mohawks, one of the tribes of the Iroquois, captured Jogues and his friend. The Mohawks killed his friend and tortured Jogues before he could escape. The Mohawks bit off Jogues' fingers, forced sticks up his wounds up to his elbow, and beat him all over his body. After his torture, he was made a slave. He then escaped and went back to France. Safely in France, Jogues chose to go back to Canada to try to convert the Indians, was captured by the Mohawks again, and this time they murdered him.

The French sent missionaries and explorers down the Mississippi River, established forts along this largest river system in North America, and laid claim to a giant territory in North America. Father Jacques Marquette and Louis Joliet explored and mapped much of the Mississippi River in the 1600s. In the late 1600s, Robert de la Salle wanted to build a huge French fur trading empire in North America. He took an exploring party and mapped the Mississippi River Valley, claiming it all for France. He named it Louisiana, in honor of the French King Louis XIV, in 1682.

Chapter 14

Founding of American Exceptionalism: Jamestown and Plymouth Plantation

The people of the young United States of America mainly spoke English, followed laws most similar to England's, mostly worshiped like the English did, and even used buildings that closely resembled England's. America would not exist without England. For us to understand the United States of America, we must understand the history of individual liberty as it developed in Great Britain. This is why this book focuses so much on this theme in the preceding chapters. However, not until Englishmen took their traditions and planted them in the soil of North America did American exceptionalism take hold in the new land. The English political tradition needed the great expanse of North America and the distance between Great Britain and the English colonists to create the opportunity for individual liberty to flourish as never before in history.

The first English attempt to found a colony in North America was by Sir Walter Raleigh in 1585, and it ended in mystery. Queen Elizabeth I granted Sir Raleigh a royal charter to establish a colony in America to find gold and riches for Great Britain. Raleigh started a colony named Roanoke in present-day North Carolina. After establishing a settlement, Governor John White left for England for supplies. Returning three years later, Governor White found no trace of the 115 colonists he had left behind; only the word "CROATOAN" was engraved on a tree. Croatoan was the name of one of the Indian tribes and a nearby island. No one knows what happened to this lost colony.

Jamestown and Plymouth Plantation give us the story of how two English colonies began in America, but also show us how the beginning of the

United States of America was exceptional, formed by religious faith and free market principles. Jamestown was founded primarily by people who risked their lives for better economic opportunities in a largely unknown place. It was financed by investors who pooled their money together to form a corporation. Plymouth Plantation was founded mainly by religious people who wanted to practice their faith in their own way, out of reach of Great Britain's religious restrictions. In both colonies, the settlers faced unbelievable hardships and suffered greatly. During the first few years, both colonies were run on a communal model, with the land owned by one company and the work and profits shared by all, regardless of individual effort and accomplishment. After each colony faced utter defeat, with over half dying in the first years, the leaders of both colonies decided to leave the communal model and give each settler his own land, and each settler then profited individually from his own labor. This change saved both Jamestown and Plymouth Plantation. Both of these colonies faced complete failure, and both decided on the same remedy that brought them success—free market principles.

JAMESTOWN

The first successful English colony in North America was the 1607 settlement of Jamestown, in the colony of Virginia. Seeing the riches Spain was taking from North and South America, the English wanted to join in. But instead of being led by the English government, the English colonies received their start from private citizens, through a type of business called a joint-stock company. Individual investors founded the London Company in 1607 and received approval from King James I to found a settlement in Virginia. The company chose a governor and colonists were employees. Most were gold-seeking gentlemen adventurers who thought physical labor beneath them. When they arrived in April, flowers bloomed along the James River, but the settlers took months to decide on a place to build a settlement, and by then it was too late for them to plant crops.

Instead of a paradise, the land of America was a nightmare for the first settlers of Jamestown. Out of 120 colonists, more than two-thirds died the first winter. They died of malnutrition, malaria, other diseases, and brackish water, and were attacked by Indians who viewed the English as another tribe to oppose. In 1608, Captain John Smith assumed control of Jamestown and imposed military discipline. He made this rule, "He who will not work will not eat." Smith organized raids on Indians, which brought the settlers food, but also more hatred toward them. But in the second winter, in 1608, less than 15% of the settlers died. After that winter, Smith was injured and sent back to England.

In the winter of 1609, the settlers experienced the harshest conditions imaginable. The London Company, now called the Virginia Company, had sent ships from England bringing people and supplies, increasing the population to nearly 500. There was not enough food for the people, and the Indians, intent on destroying the new settlement, attacked anyone who stepped outside. Settlers ate everything possible that winter, known as the Starving Time. Their meals were rats, mice, snakes, toadstools, horses, and even dead humans. When a supply ship arrived in the spring of 1610, only 60 of the 490 settlers were still alive.

For the next five years, Sir Thomas Dale, a cruel and exacting man, led Jamestown. He drove away some of the Indians and built fortifications. He punished settlers for not working hard enough by whippings and putting them to work in irons (chains) for years. Those who rebelled were executed by being tortured, starved to death, or burned to death.

Pocahontas is perhaps the most well-known of the Indians during the beginning of Jamestown. She was one of Chief Powhatan's hundred (or hundreds) of children, but reportedly his favorite. As a child, Pocahontas had played with the boys within Jamestown. When she was a young woman of 16, English Captain Samuel Argall paid Indian Chief Japazaws a copper kettle to capture her. The Jamestown settlers held Pocahontas captive so Chief Powhatan would stop attacking the settlers. In Jamestown, Pocahontas chose to become a Christian and was baptized. John Rolfe married her, they had a son, and Pocahontas went to England, where she was treated as a princess. On her return voyage to America, Pocahontas died of tuberculosis.

Tobacco

The first settlers of Jamestown believed they would find gold treasures that matched or surpassed those found by the Spanish among the Aztecs and Incas, but there was little or no gold to be found. However, the Indians introduced them to a plant that came to be the moneymaker of Virginia and other southern colonies—tobacco. Tobacco is an addictive stimulant that can be sniffed, chewed, or smoked. It soon became very popular in Europe, and was a very popular drug in America until the 1980s.

The Great Charter of Virginia

In November of 1618, everything changed for the people of Jamestown and the Virginia Colony when the Virginia Company granted a "Great Charter" to the people living in Virginia. Before the Great Charter, a common warehouse fed and clothed everyone, which was a disincentive to work because the laziest man received the same amount as the most industrious. There was never enough food, and life was harsh under the military laws, making Virginia a very unpopular place to go.

Under the new Great Charter of Virginia, the colonists were allowed a voice in their government. Virginia was granted a governor, a council, and a general assembly. The property holders of Virginia elected the general assembly, known as the House of Burgesses. It was the first group of elected lawmakers in North American history. In 1623, the Virginia Company went bankrupt, and after that the King of England chose the governor and the council. Virginia had the freest people in the world, outside of England. Everywhere else, a ruler dictated to the people what they had to do. In Jamestown, free government in America was born.

The Great Charter of Virginia also contained major changes involving private property and how an individual could support himself. It divided the land of Virginia into farms, and each man received the right to own land and work for himself. Immediately, industrious people in Virginia set out to work, and their colony saw huge improvements in its economy. Virginia became an attraction for many English people. In England, land was scarce and extremely expensive, and in Virginia, every owner of land had the right to vote. These two aspects made Virginia, and America, exceptions to the worldwide rule. Nowhere else could a person of humble means own land, prosper, and vote.

In 1619, one year after the Great Charter, two major social changes came to Virginia. Women arrived, and slave traders brought African slaves. Unlike the French, the English colonists normally would not marry Indian women. The arrival of English females meant the colony would grow on its own. To marry, a man had to gain consent from a woman, and then he had to pay her passage from England with 150 pounds of tobacco. With the arrival of slaves began the divisive slave issue in America that ended with the Civil War over two hundred years later.

PLYMOUTH PLANTATION AND THE FIRST THANKSGIVING

In the early 1600s, a group of people called Pilgrims left England to find a new home where they could practice their religion freely. In England, the government persecuted everyone who was not a member of the Church of England (Anglican). The Pilgrims were Protestants but not Anglicans. They went to Holland, where there was religious freedom.

In Holland, the Pilgrims could practice their religion freely, but they were not happy. Their children were learning to speak Dutch, practice Dutch customs, and were losing their English identity. Also, in England, the Pilgrims had been farmers, but in Holland, they lived in cities. Because of these reasons, the Pilgrims decided to leave Holland.

After returning to England for a short time, the Pilgrims left for America in 1620. The King of England had allowed them to settle in Virginia. While at sea, a storm hit, and they sailed off course, over 600 miles north of Jamestown. After traveling 65 days, they landed their ship, the Mayflower, in the

New World. Before stepping ashore, they wrote the Mayflower Compact, a short paper declaring every person's intention to glorify God, follow the laws, and to honor the King of England. They wanted to make it clear to the king they were not intentionally founding a settlement far from Virginia. The Mayflower Compact was the first self-written constitution in North America. 102 English citizens set foot in America and founded Plymouth, in present-day Massachusetts. The Pilgrims stayed on their ship until they could build homes out of the wood from the forest.

At Plymouth Plantation, the first year was incredibly harsh for the Pilgrims. They settled on abandoned Indian fields. Of the 102 settlers, 45 died within a few months. Of the 18 women, only 4 survived that first year. The Pilgrims were unaccustomed to the harsh winters of the Northeast, and did not know which crops grew best. Afraid of the Indians, who had attacked a Pilgrim exploring party, the Pilgrims leveled and planted corn over the graves when they buried their dead. They did this so the Indians would not know how weak the Pilgrims were.

One day in spring, an Indian man named Samoset walked up to the Pilgrims, and to their surprise, said, "Welcome, Englishmen." Samoset had learned English from English fishermen, who travelled to the American coast for the abundant fishing. He introduced the Pilgrims to Squanto, who had lived among English speakers for a time as a slave. When Squanto regained his freedom, he went back to his people in America. Squanto taught the Pilgrims what crops to grow and how to use fish as a fertilizer. He also acted as a peaceful contact between the Pilgrims and the most powerful Indian of the area, Chief Massasoit.

In the fall of 1621, the Pilgrims, a very religious people, decided to set aside a time to honor God and give him thanks for all of their blessings. It is amazing to think of the faith, courage, and humility of these people. In a year, half of them had died in a cold and cruel climate. They were far from their friends and comforts. And still, they wanted to set aside several days to give

God thanks for their blessings. They invited their neighbors, the Indians, to show them thanks for their help, and to include them in their feast.

The first Thanksgiving in America lasted for three days, involved all of the Pilgrims (approximately 50), and 90 Indian men. It is believed the Indian women did not attend because the Indians did not trust the Englishmen. In the Indian culture of the Northeast, it was common for Indians to steal the wives of enemies, and the Indians thought the Pilgrims would do the same to them. During these three days, the Indians played competitive games, and the English and Indian men shared the best foods together.

Two years later, in 1623, the governor of Massachusetts, William Bradford, wrote America's first Thanksgiving Proclamation. He set aside a specific day and time for the citizens to honor God for his blessings. Beginning with President George Washington, U.S. presidents have issued a Thanksgiving Proclamation as well. In 1863, in the middle of the American Civil War, during which over 600,000 Americans were killed, President Abraham Lincoln declared that the last Thursday in November be set aside as "a day of Thanksgiving and Praise to our beneficent Father who dwelleth in the Heavens." Lincoln's proclamation made Thanksgiving Day a federal holiday.

In Plymouth Plantation, just as in Jamestown, the settlers first tried to share everything, including land, work, clothing, food and drink. But, as in Jamestown, there were always shortages, and there were those who would not work and so benefitted from the work of others. In 1624, each family received its own land, and from that time on, Plymouth Plantation was a success. The industrious worked hard, saved, and grew in wealth and in self-sufficiency.

Primary Source Documents from Plymouth Plantation
The Mayflower Compact
1620

In the name of God, Amen. We whose names are under-written, the loyal subjects of our dread sovereign Lord, King James, by the grace of God, of Great Britain, France, and Ireland King, Defender of the Faith, etc.

Having undertaken, for the glory of God, and advancement of the Christian faith, and honor of our King and Country, a voyage to plant the first colony in the northern parts of Virginia, do by these presents solemnly and mutually, in the presence of God, and one of another, covenant and combine our selves together into a civil body politic, for our better ordering and preservation and furtherance of the ends aforesaid; and by virtue hereof to enact, constitute, and frame such just and equal laws, ordinances, acts, constitutions and offices, from time to time, as shall be thought most meet and convenient for the general good of the Colony, unto which we promise all due submission and obedience. In witness whereof we have hereunder subscribed our names at Cape Cod, the eleventh of November [New Style, November 21], in the year of the reign of our sovereign lord, King James, of England, France, and Ireland, the eighteenth, and of Scotland the fifty-fourth. Anno Dom. 1620.

AMERICA'S FIRST THANKSGIVING PROCLAMATION
BY GOVERNOR BRADFORD
1623

Inasmuch as the great Father has given us this year an abundant harvest of Indian corn, wheat, peas, beans, squashes, and garden vegetables, and has made the forests to abound with game and the sea with fish and clams, and inasmuch as he has protected us from the ravages of the savages, has spared us from pestilence and disease, has granted us freedom to worship God according to the dictates of our own conscience.

Now I, your magistrate, do proclaim that all ye Pilgrims, with your wives and ye little ones, do gather at ye meeting house, on ye hill, between the hours of 9 and 12 in the day time, on Thursday, November 29th, of the year of our Lord one thousand six hundred and twenty-three and the third year since ye Pilgrims landed on ye Pilgrim Rock, there to listen to ye pastor and render thanksgiving to ye Almighty God for all His blessings.

CHAPTER 15

AMERICAN EXCEPTIONALISM TAKES HOLD IN THE ENGLISH COLONIES

Over the next century and a half, from the first English colony of Jamestown in 1607 to the time the 13 English colonies rebelled against Great Britain in the American Revolution (1775-1783), a new nation was born. In some ways, this new nation looked similar to others in the world, with a common language, similar ways of living and thinking, and a geographical boundary. In other more important ways, America was different than any nation on Earth. These differences form the main reason for what some historians correctly call "American Exceptionalism." American exceptionalism means that in its founding and throughout its history, the United States of America has been the exception to the rule.

We can see at least eight elements of American Exceptionalism in the English colonies of the 1600s and 1700s.
1. Limited, Representative Democracy
2. Constitutionalism
3. Protestant Christian Heritage and the Birth of Religious Freedom
4. Militia System
5. Free Market Principles, Private Property, and Availability of Land
6. Abundant Natural Resources
7. Rebellion Against an Unpopular Government
8. Accessible Education

LIMITED, REPRESENTATIVE DEMOCRACY

In most of the colonies, the government consisted of a governor and council appointed by the King of England, and a legislature and judiciary elected by citizens of the colony. The first legislature in colonial America was the Virginia House of Burgesses. The American Founding Fathers recognized the legislature as the most important branch of government. The legislature makes laws and taxes citizens. The fact that English colonists could choose their lawmakers is exceptional. This represented the greatest political participation of people in the world. In no other country did average people have the right to vote.

Some may argue that it was unfair that slaves, free blacks, women, and at first men who did not own land could not vote. If we judge history by today's values, that is true. However, this is not a fair comparison. In the 1600s, throughout the world, only those lucky enough to be born into a royal family, or who took power violently, could participate in government. Compared with this fact, the English colonists were the freest people in the world.

Constitutionalism

Constitutionalism is a set of ideas, attitudes, and behavior based on the principle that the authority of government comes from a body of fundamental law. It means that government is limited by its laws and the practices of law and government over a period of time. The rule of law is another concept that is part of constitutionalism. The rule of law means that a country is governed not by the opinions and whims of its rulers, but by written laws. Constitutionalism and the rule of law are two concepts that make it impossible for a ruler to take full control of a government.

In the English colonies, each colony had a written charter, with the laws of the colony specifically written. No official was above the law. In 1639, for instance, colonists wrote the Fundamental Orders of Connecticut. This document explained how the government of Connecticut would work, describing the powers and limits of the government.

Protestant Christian Heritage and the Birth of Religious Freedom

The English colonists practiced their strong religious beliefs on a daily basis. Most colonists were very strong Christians, read the Bible as families, individually, and in churches, and tried to follow God's will in everything they did. American Protestant Christians believed in working hard and that every person should be able to read and understand the Bible. In large part because of this, colonial America became a big success, and literacy was widespread.

In most of the colonies and in Europe of the 1600s, there was an established state church. Virginia required Anglican membership. Massachusetts required Puritan membership. Those of other faiths could not live in these colonies. As in Europe, church attendance was mandatory, and people were fined if they did not attend. In some colonies, individuals could be publicly beaten for not following the established church.

Three English colonies led the way in establishing freedom of religion: Rhode Island, Maryland, and Pennsylvania. Each of these colonies was founded by people who disagreed with the Anglican Church, but who did not want to persecute peoples of other faiths. Roger Williams, banished from Massachusetts for his beliefs that went counter to the official Puritan colonial religion, founded Rhode Island as a colony where an individual could practice any religion he chose. William Penn, a Quaker, founded Pennsylvania and established religious freedom there. Lord Baltimore, a Roman Catholic, founded Maryland (the Land of Mary) and for a time in Maryland each colonist had religious freedom. Religious freedom ended in Maryland after the Glorious Revolution, 1688-1689, when Protestants established the Anglican Church and expelled Jesuits, thus forcing Catholics to practice their faith clandestinely.

Religious freedom was born in the American colonies for a number of reasons. Many colonists left Europe for the express purpose of practicing their own religion. Once in America, some colonists did enjoy religious freedom, but others did not. Nevertheless, by the time the U.S. Constitution was ratified in 1789, Americans realized that life was better for everyone without an established church. Those who faced persecution did not want to persecute others.

Militia System

In the 1600s and for most of the 1700s, the colonists developed a military mindset and a number of practices that historian Daniel Boorstin described as the militia system. This mindset continues in a transformed way in America today. English colonists had a distrust of a king's standing army, but needed to protect themselves from Indians. Each man aged 16-60 was expected to have his own gun and ammunition, and if he lived in a village or town, he was expected to volunteer and train for a potential war. Once the war ended, it was expected that he would return to his farm to work, and there would be no standing army. No one earned a permanent salary for military service.

The militia system operated throughout the colonies, though there was little communication between them. When the colonists fought the Indians, they engaged them with a "western way of war" that proved most effective. Daniel Boorstin wrote that the Americans borrowed Indian guerilla warfare tactics and combined them with European tactics like volleys. Guerilla warfare tactics include ambushing superior forces when they divide, attacking supply lines, and "hit and run" tactics, or using the environment as cover. In addition, there was equality, or at least a heightened mutual respect, among commanders and troops. This relationship helped commanders listen to soldiers on the battlefield and change tactics, if necessary.

Free Market Principles and Availability of Private Property

Free market principles are ways of thinking and acting that allow each individual to determine what is best and to freely work toward the ends he wants. Private property is an essential part of the free market because each person can strive to own his own farm or business, and reap the rewards from his labors.

At the founding of the first two colonies, Jamestown and Plymouth Plantation, the land was held by a company, and each colonist shared everything.

This meant that the laziest person received the same amount of food and goods as the hardest working. When this system failed miserably, bringing great destruction and death, the leaders of both colonies decided to allow the colonists to own their own land, and to benefit from their own hard work. Once these reforms occurred, both Jamestown and Plymouth Plantation became successful.

Throughout the 13 English colonies, individuals could own land. Nowhere else in the world was this similar. In most places, landowners had to be born into a royal family. This unmatched right to own private property drew many Europeans to settle in the English colonies, and it was a major reason why the English colonies became so prosperous.

Abundant Natural Resources

When Englishmen first came to America, they expected to find gold. Of course, they did not. However, what they found was perhaps more valuable than gold. America's vast natural resources were unparalleled in the world. Nowhere else was there so much open land, with varied climate, soil, and minerals. The American Indians did occupy North America, but they were not everywhere, and in many places, Indians were nomads. European settlers found much open land to call home, and they won land from Indians by military victory or by treaties.

Rebellion Against an Unpopular Government

In at least two instances, the English colonists of the 1600s rebelled against the government. Nathaniel Bacon of Virginia led the first revolt. Bacon and many Virginians were angry at Governor Berkeley for not providing enough protection against the Indians. Bacon and about 1,000 rebels rose against the governor, chased him from Jamestown, and burned the capital city. Bacon caught a sickness and died, and the rebellion was put down, but the King recalled the governor to England. Bacon's Rebellion showed how the English colonists were willing to fight against the royal government.

The second instance American colonists opposed the government was during the English Glorious Revolution, 1688-1689. The English did not like King James II because he was Catholic and had issued a Toleration Act, allowing English people to be Anglican or Catholic. In America, King James II took away all New England royal charters and tried to establish one central colonial government in Boston. Colonists resisted with force. Colonists overthrew King James' government in America, and forced the king to surrender the colonies back to their original colonial governments. In England, the English overthrew King James II and established William and Mary as rulers. Catholics were persecuted in England after the Glorious Revolution.

Parliament asked the Protestant daughter of King James II, Mary, and her husband William, to rule England, after they agreed to the Declaration of Rights. Some of the rights in this declaration closely resemble the American Bill of Rights created only 100 years later. The following are a few of these rights:

1. Monarch was not supreme but shared authority with Parliament and the courts
2. House of Commons was the source of all revenue bills (power of the purse)
3. Right to free speech and petition
4. Due process of law
5. No excessive punishment
6. No standing army during peacetime and the right of English Protestants to keep and bear arms

Soon thereafter, Whig John Locke advocated in his Two Treatises that all men are born free, equal, and rational, and entitled to the God-given rights of life, liberty, and property.

Accessible Education

For education, colonists of the 1600s learned nearly exclusively in the home. Because the great majority of colonists were Puritans, Anglicans (members of the Anglican Church) or other Protestant religions, parents felt it necessary to teach children how to read and understand the Bible. As the Old Testament and New Testament in the Bible are challenging, most English settlers had a good command of reading. At the time of the American Revolution, Americans were among the best educated people in the world.

Chapter 16

Commonalities of Life in the English Colonies

For most colonists, the first decades of life in the new English colonies were extremely difficult. However, the fact that Englishmen kept coming to North America is proof that life in America was better, or that Englishmen had greater hope for the future living in America than in England.

Life in the Home and Travel

When new settlers arrived, they often dug the first houses in the ground. During winters, it was warmer underneath than above the ground. Then, as time and work allowed, they built rude cabins of round logs with a dirt floor. Later, bigger houses were built with a large room in the middle, called a hall. Houses had large chimneys with wide fireplaces that children could put chairs in to look at the stars at night. Of course, this was when there was no fire burning! The first windows in English America were made of oiled paper (so light could come through). Settlers made their own furniture and beds filled with wild pigeon feathers, mistletoe, and down from cattail flags. The first English Americans used knifes and ate on wooden plates with their fingers, as utensils were a luxury. Only the very rich had silverware.

The wealthier colonists wore linen, wool, lace, and silver buckles. Ordinary colonists wore clothing made in the home by the women of the household. Working men wore wool, leather, deerskin, or coarse canvas breeches.

Women cooked in the fireplace, by placing the meat on an iron rod and turning it by crank, or by boiling or cooking in pots, skillets and on griddles that stood upon legs. Colonists drank beer at all meals, because beer is brewed (boiled), which kills disease in water. For food, colonists ate bread and cheese, and porridge of peas and beans, with a little meat. They made mush from Indian corn for dinner. No tea or coffee was known in the colonies or in England until the late 1600s. Colonists often drank alcohol, including corn whiskey, rum and peach brandy.

The fastest form of travel until the mid-1800s was by water. People often travelled in canoes, with some canoes holding 40 people. No roads existed for nearly the first 100 years of colonization. To travel by foot or on horse, colonists used Indian trails.

WORK IN THE COLONIES

Over 90% of English settlers were farmers. With land abundant in America, colonists took great pride in owning and running their own farms. Most boys in farming families grew up to be farmers, like their fathers. In towns, a boy of 14 often became an apprentice to a Master in a trade. An apprentice would enter into a legal contract with a Master for usually four to seven years. The apprentice lived in the Master's house, learned his trade, and worked for his education, room and board. He also promised to never reveal his Master's secrets. At the end of his apprenticeship, the apprentice was expected to become a Master of the trade. Colonial tradesmen included blacksmiths, silversmiths, apothecaries (druggists), basket makers, brick makers, cabinetmakers, milliners, printers and binders, shoemakers, tailors, coopers (barrel makers), wigmakers, gunsmiths, and founders. There were also indentured servants and slaves, which are discussed later.

All free men in the English colonies had an incredible amount of opportunity, which gave them great hope and excitement. Nowhere else in the world could a common man own land and run his own farm or become a Master of a trade through hard work and determination. Elsewhere, for example in Europe, it was more important which family a person came from than how hard a person worked.

GIRLS AND WOMEN IN COLONIAL AMERICA

Because of the huge challenges of physical survival in colonial America, and the physical nature of most work, as well as the multiple intelligences required to feed, clothe, and run a household, women managed the entire household, and brought up girls to be educators of children, conveyors of culture and morality, and capable seamstresses, cooks, business managers, and partners with their husbands. Much has been misunderstood about the importance and honor given to women in colonial America. To her husband and children, she was the source of life, responsible for feeding and clothing the family, and she saw to the transmission of culture through education. One way to look at it is that she ruled the household, and her husband and children were her servants, looking to her for guidance, for daily sustenance, and for love. Unmarried women or widows had property rights, but married women did not unless there was a trust or pre-nuptial agreement. None could vote.

Laws in the Colonies

Many laws in the colonies reflected the Puritan population's beliefs involving a person's morality and relationship to church. There were laws against lying, using profane language and not going to church. In Boston on Sundays, 100 years after Plymouth Plantation's founding, no walking was allowed except to go to church, and no sitting was allowed in Boston Common. Women were punished for scolding by being tied up to a chair and dunked into water. Drunkards had to wear a red letter D around their necks or had to stand with their head and hands in the pillory, while other people threw eggs at them. Other punishments included whipping on the bare back, cropping the ears, branding the hand with a hot iron, and hanging in chains. Although these punishments seem harsh to us today, they were the same as in Europe.

Slavery

One sad fact of life in the 1600s was slavery. Slavery has existed since the beginning of man in nearly all countries of the world, so it was not different or exceptional that the English colonists had slaves. In the colonies, the South practiced slavery more than anywhere else because of the geography and climate. Tobacco and rice grew well in the South and both required much labor. Early poor white settlers were indentured servants, obligated to work hard for five to seven years by contract. But by the 1700s, white indentured servitude was ending. After the American Revolution, the North outlawed slavery, but it remained the greatest difference between the South and the rest of the country. Eventually, Americans would fight a Civil War to end slavery.

Chapter 17

Southern Colonies

English colonization in North America began in the South, and at the time of the American Revolution, the Southern colonies had a larger population and economy than the rest of the county. American Founding Fathers George Washington, Thomas Jefferson, James Madison, and Patrick Henry all came from Virginia, perhaps the most important colony, alongside Massachusetts.

The Southern colonies were Georgia, South Carolina, North Carolina, Virginia, and Maryland. The first settlers of Virginia never did find gold, but what they did find became almost as valuable. Indians introduced the Jamestown colonists to tobacco. The English quickly fell in love with the plant that they could smoke or sniff, and tobacco became the currency for most of the settlers in Virginia. If a settler wanted to buy something, he would pay in pounds of tobacco! Without tobacco, the settlement of Virginia and perhaps the success of the English colonies might not have happened.

Climate in the Southern colonies was warm and humid in the summer and mild in the winter, ideal for farming. Broad rivers made it easy to bring crops to market. There are few high mountains and the Appalachian Mountains reach no higher than a few thousand feet. The main crops of the South were tobacco, rice, and indigo. In the backcountry beyond the farms, Southerners hunted wild animals.

The Southern colonies started for various reasons. The London Company founded Virginia to make a profit for its investors. Lord Baltimore established Maryland as a place for Catholics and people of all faiths to worship freely. King Charles II founded North and South Carolina to keep the French and Spanish away. Georgia was founded by James Oglethorpe, who convinced King George II to allow debtors in English prisons to settle in

Georgia, work, and pay off their debt. So when historians write that Georgia was founded by prisoners, they are telling the truth!

Nearly every Southerner worked on a farm. The great majority of white Southern families owned individual small farms. About 5% of Southerners were rich plantation owners. A plantation was a huge farm, where a hundred or more slaves would labor. About 35%-45% of the Southern colonies' population was slave.

For recreation, Southern whites spent their time horse racing, hunting, dancing, card playing or playing the violin or flute. Children played many games during their free time. In the game "rolling the hoop," each child would roll a wooden hoop and race to a finish line, trying to reach it first. Another game, "pins," was very much like our game of bowling. Children played marbles, hopscotch, leapfrog, and tag.

Chapter 18

New England Colonies

New England is home to Boston, probably the most important city at the beginning of the American Revolution. Boston is where the Boston Massacre took place and where the colonists dumped tea into the harbor, the so-called Boston Tea Party. And, it was in Boston that General Washington enjoyed his first major military success against the British.

The New England colonies were New Hampshire, Massachusetts, Connecticut, and Rhode Island. Important Bostonians of the American Revolution include Paul Revere, Samuel Adams, John Adams, and John Hancock. The American Revolution started right outside of Boston, at the towns of Lexington and Concord, in 1775.

New England climate is cold, wet, and continental (having four seasons). It is an area with many small mountains, making it challenging for colonists to have large farms. The small mountains and snows, however, create many streams, which helped later during the Industrial Revolution because small mills (factories) run by water could be built in New England. Dairy farms run by small, independent families, fur trapping, and ocean-going trades such as ship-building, fishing, and whaling, were the main industries of New England.

In 1629, a decade after the Pilgrims arrived, the Massachusetts Bay Colony received a charter. The company elected a General Court, which chose a governor named John Winthrop, and assistants. When Winthrop and 11 ships arrived in Massachusetts, he said, "Wee must Consider that wee shall be as a City upon a Hill, the eyes of all people are upon us." Winthrop believed that something exceptional was being created in America, and he wanted to create a place where God's rules would lead society.

Called the Moses of the Puritans, Winthrop led the Great Migration to North America. From 1629 to 1640, more than 20,000 Puritans left England for Massachusetts. In England, anyone who was not an Anglican (a member of the Anglican Church) faced persecution. Still, the King of England allowed the Puritans to leave for America and allowed them to establish their own rule there.

The Puritans opposed rituals, emphasized preaching, and strongly opposed anything that resembled the Catholic Church. Though the Puritans left England to worship freely, they kept with the practices of the 1600s, and forbade all other forms of religious worship in Massachusetts. In fact, a man had to prove himself a Puritan in good standing in order to vote. On one hand, this was the freest form of democracy in the world at that time. All Puritan men could participate in elections. On the other hand, if you were a Catholic or a Jew, you had to leave the colony. The Puritans outnumbered and overpowered the original Pilgrim settlers.

Thomas Hooker, a Puritan in Massachusetts, wanted citizens to have greater participation in politics. He led a number of Puritans away and founded the colony of Connecticut. The Fundamental Orders of Connecticut, a document created by Hooker, describes the type of government in that colony. It limits the power of political leaders by requiring all leaders to be elected and prevents an absolute ruler through balanced branches of government.

New England was an area of small farmers who lived near towns. Because of the cold weather, crops that required greater sun did poorly, and farms did not need as much labor as in the South. Perhaps this is why slavery did not take hold in the North. People in New England were known for working very hard.

New England had less recreation than the South. The Puritans did not permit card playing or dancing, both seen as sinful practices. Girls played with homemade dolls and boys played marbles, or played soldiers by marching or shooting their guns. People hunted to bring food home, but hunting also provided entertainment.

Puritans are famous in America for having strict rules. One interesting Puritan custom was their tradition of dating. As soon as a young man could afford a farm and support a family, possibly at the age of 19, he could court a girl who was at least age 13. For a "date," the boy had to ask permission from the girl's father. Typically, the first part of the date was a dinner at the girl's house. Then, if the boy and girl went outside for a walk during the "date," the entire girl's family had to follow the boy and girl wherever they went. When a boy and girl eventually decided they wanted to marry, one thing they did was "bundling". The boy was sewn shut (except his head) inside a potato sack, and he and the girl went to sleep in the same bed. The next morning, if the sack was not broken, and the boy and the girl still wanted to, they could marry.

As in all the colonies, religion was extremely important. In Massachusetts in the 1600s, each citizen had to be a Puritan. All others could not live within the state. Roger Williams, pastor of a Massachusetts church, preached against traditional Puritan teachings. He believed that no one should be forced to be religious, and that it was impossible to determine if someone were saved. Massachusetts banned Roger Williams, and he was forced to go into an area of land where only Indians lived. Williams made friends with the Indians and started the colony of Rhode Island as a place with complete religious freedom.

The church was the largest building in New England towns, and all had to attend, as in Europe. Someone skipping church service could be punished with a fine or with physical punishment in the middle of town. During church services, a designated person kept the boys and men awake by poking them with a stick or using a feather to tickle them.

In the 1600s, throughout Europe and America, people believed that witches practiced witchcraft, placing spells on individuals or towns. On both continents, if the government believed you were a witch, you could be tortured and executed. In Salem, Massachusetts, a group of girls accused many townspeople of being witches. To save themselves from execution, the accused only had to admit their guilt and ask forgiveness. None of the accused would admit to being witches because they were truly Christians. In 1693, 20 were executed and 7 died in prison. This incident, known as the Salem Witch Trials, was the first and last incident of this kind in America.

Chapter 19

The Middle Colonies

The Middle Colonies of New York, Pennsylvania, New Jersey, and Delaware were settled last. They were nicknamed "the bread colonies" because of their extremely rich soil and great climate for crops, both fruits and vegetables. Sheep, cattle, dairy products, wool, and food were plentiful. Important rivers went inland and provided farmers with transportation links to the coast and to important trading cities such as Philadelphia and New York.

In the 1600s, the Holland Trading Company hired Englishman Henry Hudson, in the ship the Half Moon, to find the Northwest Passage. Europeans continued to falsely believe that there was an all-water route through America to the Pacific Ocean. Hudson explored rivers in what was to become the Middle Colonies. He named a river the River of Mountains, later renamed the Hudson River. Settlers from Holland continued to arrive and founded New Netherlands. In 1664, the English took this land from Holland and renamed it New York City.

New York Governor Thomas Dongan was born in Ireland in 1634. An Irish Catholic, he faced severe religious and political oppression from England, where the practice of Catholicism was forbidden and, at times, punishable by torture and death. In New York, he made certain that all people would enjoy freedoms that were written down and protected by the government. In the mid-1600s, Dongan established the New York Assembly, which passed the Charter of Liberties. The Charter of Liberties guaranteed its citizens three things that would later become part of U.S. Constitution:
    1. Trial by jury
    2. Right to vote on certain questions
    3. Religious freedom

Pennsylvania was one of the first colonies, after Rhode Island, founded on the idea of religious freedom. Its founder, William Penn, belonged to the Society of Friends, a religious group also known as the Quakers. Quakers did not believe in titles or nobility or fighting in war, they believed all people to be friends, and they dressed plainly. Penn was expelled from Oxford University in England because he would not wear the cap and gown of the student, and because the Friends tried to tear the caps and gowns off their classmates. The king owed William Penn's father a debt, and when his father died, William asked the king for a land grant to start a colony in America. Penn founded Pennsylvania in 1681, and the city of Philadelphia (meaning brotherly love in Latin) the next year. Penn made a treaty with the Indians in the area, and established a colony where no one had to practice any religion. Settlers rushed into Pennsylvania from England, but also from Scotland, Ireland, and Germany. Americans called Pennsylvania the "Keystone State" because it is the middle or key state on the Atlantic coast.

Chapter 20

Early Indian Wars

Immediately after Europeans moved to America, Indians and settlers fought each other. In Jamestown in 1607, Indians attacked the settlers within days of their arrival. Throughout the 1600s and 1700s, atrocities occurred on both sides, as Indians saw the European settlers as another tribe to defeat, and as European settlers sought to gain control over North America. Some warlike Indian tribes in the eastern part of America had ways of fighting that shocked the Europeans. The settlers relied on their increasing manpower, superior weaponry, and military philosophy to gain victory.

In 1622, in Jamestown, Virginia, a long war began when Indians massacred 347 men, women, and children. Chief Opechankano, who had led the first massacre, planned a second. So old he could not walk without assistance, and blind unless others held open his eyelids, he was led to the fight. On that day, Indians killed over 500 settlers. By 1644, however, English settlers had grown in strength, and they finally put down the Indians, eventually capturing Opechankano, who was killed by an enraged soldier.

Considerable animosity grew between the Indians and the English in many of the colonies. The Indians of the Northeast had a warrior society, where it was not acceptable to be captured by the enemy. If an enemy tribe captured a man, he expected to be slowly tortured until death. Babies caught in battle were immediately killed, and in some cases, were cooked and eaten. However, Indians sometimes adopted children and welcomed them into their families. Captured women and girls were made slaves or wives, and were brutalized the rest of their lives. Since this was how Indians treated other Indians from enemy tribes, it was how they treated the English as well. Many English colonists reacted to the Indian way of war by wanting to exterminate all Indians.

In Connecticut, in 1634-1638, English settlers fought against the Pequot tribe. Indians, being light of foot, could run away from English warriors, who wore medieval armor. The Indians brutally tortured and murdered captured Englishmen. At Mystic, Connecticut, just before morning, English settlers surrounded a Pequot village, set it on fire, and shot or burned to death over 500 Indians. After this incident, there were no other Indian wars in New England for some time.

During the 1640s and 1650s, brutal wars took place throughout the other English colonies between the Indians and the English settlers. Fighting and raids happened between the Dutch settlers and the Indians in what is now New York, and between the Marylanders and the Susquehannah tribe. Where Richmond, Virginia is today, Indians defeated Virginians at the Battle of Bloody Run, a brook given that name because the blood of the English made the water turn red.

Fifty-five years after the Pilgrims landed at Plymouth Plantation and shared a meal with the Indians, King Phillip's War took place. Phillip (whose Indian name was Metacom) was the son of Massasoit, the chief in control of the area the Pilgrims originally inhabited. Metacom had initially been friendly with the English, and took the name of King Phillip. He was, however, angered that Puritan English settlers were expanding, and that many Indians from Phillip's tribe were converting to Christianity. The "Apostle to the Indians" John Eliot had translated the Bible into the local Indian language and had converted whole villages, which upset many Indian religious leaders, known as medicine men. Three Indians murdered a Christian Indian, and for their crime, were hung in Massachusetts Colony. In response, King Phillip launched an attack on colonial towns.

During the war, Indians caused tremendous damage and harm to New Englanders, and New Englanders caused great death and calamity to Indians. Indians attacked more than half of New England towns and killed over 10% of the male population. New Englanders killed more than 2,000 Indians in war and sold 1,000 Indians into slavery. In addition, 3,000 Indians died through sickness and starvation. For many years after the official end of the war, English colonists were faced with hostile Indians throughout the frontier. English colonists became determined to rid themselves of all Indians within their territories, and called on Great Britain to help.

In Virginia and South Carolina, settlers fought more wars against the Indians. In Virginia, Nathaniel Bacon organized a war party to fight the Indians. Further south, the Tuscarora, and later, the Yamassee, tried to completely destroy the colony of South Carolina.

When the European settlers came, the primary Indian weapon was the bow and arrow. The arrow had as its head a sharp flint rock or the claw of an eagle. After this weapon, the Indian used a war-club and a tomahawk, a club with a stone ax fixed to it. Once the Indians realized the power of a gun or of European knives and hatchets, they gave up their weapons for the better ones.

Initially, European settlers used matchlock guns. These weapons had to be rested on a long stick because they were so heavy. They had to be fired by first lighting a fuse, and the shooter could not move or he would miss. In the 1670s, settlers started to use the flintlock gun, which fired much faster. When pulling the trigger, the flint would strike steel and let off a spark that would ignite the gun.

Settlers learned that when fighting Indians, they had to employ different tactics than those used in fighting enemies in Europe. For one, during winter, settlers learned about using snowshoes, so, instead of sinking in the snow, they could walk on top of snow, just like Indians did. Also, settlers learned to march in single file, to lie in ambush, and to load their guns while concealed, lying down or behind trees.

Throughout the wars with Indians, English settlers became adept at fighting a vicious foe in the wilderness. The fight not only involved men, but included the entire family. Women and children had to know how to defend themselves by using weapons and forming military units, and in the process, they endured years of fear and the unknown. The Indians forced the English colonists to be strong, independent, and confident American people.

UNIT IV

FOUNDING OF THE U.S.A.

Introduction

It is fitting that the individual acts of thousands of common Americans ignited the American Revolution in the fields, paths, forests, and small towns surrounding Boston. In 1775, a great majority of Americans were small farmers, inhabiting the countryside less than a day's ride to a city. The colonists had no standing army, no navy, no united military organization, and no official government, besides the Continental Congress that met for discussions in Philadelphia. The English colonists were not united by a ruling elite, but by a common goal of individual liberty and a growing frustration toward a distant king and Parliament that was out of touch with the American sentiment and determination for radical self-rule. Americans were driven by the ideal of a nation led by justice and equality under the law. The unavoidable fact that 20% of America was enslaved did not bother all inhabitants. Slavery had been the way of the world for time immemorial. And, there were those who wanted to end slavery, but the first step was throwing off an unelected and unrepresentative king and Parliament.

Without intelligent and virtuous leaders, however, there would have been no American Revolution. The actions and words of the American Founding Fathers have blessed Americans not just in their own lifetime, but for hundreds of years. It is hard or perhaps impossible to name another time and place where a country has had at her beginning such leaders as George Washington, John Adams, Thomas Jefferson, James Monroe, James Madison, Benjamin Franklin, Alexander Hamilton, John Marshall, Samuel Adams, Patrick Henry, and countless other leaders. Along with nearly all of these leaders were their wives who provided advice, management of home and business, and logistical support to both the Continental Army and their families.

Nearly anyone who studied the situation thought that Great Britain would win the American Revolution. The British had just defeated France and Spain, boasted the best navy in the world, had perhaps the best and most experienced officers and soldiers, and had a much stronger economy than the Americans. However, the Atlantic Ocean was a huge barrier and tactical problem for resupplying a large fighting force in America. Most fights were away from the coast, so the British often could not use their navy. George Washington also calculated that he could win the war by keeping his army intact and on the battlefield. He reasoned that if he kept his soldiers fighting long enough, the British would tire of trying to capture him, and the British public would lose interest in the war. Washington developed aggressive American officers, such as Nathaniel Greene and Ethan Allen. His envoys also convinced most Indian tribes not to join the British. Foreign fighters and officers—Marquis de Lafayette of France, Baron von Steuben of Prussia, and others—joined the Americans and provided excellent leadership. In addition, Benjamin Franklin, John Adams, and Thomas Jefferson persuaded France to eventually join the war on America's side. These factors enabled the new nation to defeat the strongest country on Earth.

CHAPTER 21

EARLY CAUSES OF THE AMERICAN REVOLUTION

From the time of the first English settlement in America through the first part of the 1760s, nearly all colonists in America considered themselves English, never thinking of breaking away from Great Britain. However, in just a few short years, the 13 colonies united in a war against the mother country, and formed their own country, the United States of America. The separation from Great Britain became official at the moment the Declaration of Independence was adopted on July 4, 1776, but this was after years of problems and differences between the Americans and the British.

THE FIRST GREAT AWAKENING (1730s AND 1740s)

Much of English America was founded by English Protestants wanting to practice their faith, free from the control of Great Britain. However, in the early 1700s, American religious leaders thought that the colonists were losing sight of what was important, their religious belief. These leaders organized large religious gatherings outdoors where preachers would exhort listeners to turn from their sinful ways, accept Jesus Christ as their savior, and to live a new life under God.

Two leaders of the First Great Awakening were Jonathan Edwards and George Whitefield. Edwards was a third generation Puritan from Connecticut, trained at Yale, who excited large numbers of people to follow Christ, reform their lives, and to become involved in public affairs. Whitefield emigrated from Great Britain and was a master showman. Both hosted open-air meetings and exhorted thousands to avoid the fires of hell. People came from miles away to listen, convert, and to camp outside among other Christians. Whitefield impersonated God and Satan on stage and presented a dramatic portrayal of the choices of salvation or damnation. At the end of the sermon, listeners would come forward, tears in their eyes, confessing their sins, and promising to live their lives for Christ.

Some common threads run throughout the First Great Awakening. Listeners were called to individually accept Jesus as their savior, religious expression was encouraged, and preachers, especially later, did not have to have official licenses to be ministers. The movement encouraged the English colonists to take responsibility over their own welfare and to rely on personal experiences to make life-altering decisions. Within 30 to 40 years, these colonists decided to break away from Great Britain. The First Great Awakening helped prepare them to do so.

French and Indian War (1754-1763)

Throughout the colonial period, England fought France in four major wars in North America. At times, Spain joined with France. Both France and England wanted to control North America and saw themselves the rightful owners. The French had a successful fur trade that the English wanted. The English were Protestant and the French were Roman Catholic. England had a limited monarchy and France had an absolute monarchy. English settlers had many more political rights than French settlers. However, perhaps the greatest difference between the English settlers and the French settlers was their number: there were 16 English for every one Frenchmen in North America in 1750 (c. 1.6 million English colonists and at most c. 100,000 French).

The French and Indian War started over control of the Ohio Valley, but ended with domination of the continent. The French established forts from Quebec to New Orleans, with fur traders active throughout the land west of Appalachian Mountains. English colonists lived up and down the Atlantic Coast on a narrow strip of land, up to 150 miles from the ocean. Once the English colonists began to cross over the Appalachians, they came into conflict with the French. The English believed they had the right to the land all the way to the Pacific Ocean.

To send the French a message that the English wanted them out of the Ohio Valley, Governor Robert Dinwiddie of Virginia sent a young and capable

21-year-old major in the Virginia militia, George Washington. Washington and his men surprised a smaller number of French soldiers. The French attempted to surrender, but Washington's Indian allies would not stop, leaving no Frenchmen alive. Washington then retreated, building Fort Necessity. A larger French force attacked with superior power, forcing Washington to surrender, but he wrote later, he "heard the bullets whistle and …there is something charming in the sound."

Throughout the war, George Washington impressed both the English and the colonists, and became recognized as a leader. In one battle, George Washington attempted to warn the British General Braddock of the danger of marching with red coats on a narrow path through the forest, and he tried to tell the British how the Indians fought in America. General Braddock dismissed the advice, and at the Battle of Monongahela, Braddock was killed, along with every other officer except Washington. Washington had multiple horses shot from under him, had bullets pierce his vest, yet he still ably led the British in an organized retreat.

Great Britain defeated France in the French and Indian War, and in the Treaty of Paris in 1763, received all of the French territory in North America. This meant that Great Britain now controlled all of Canada and the land east of the Mississippi River, and north of Florida and Louisiana. Colonists went home, hoping to return to life without war. As the English moved into the French forts west of the Appalachian Mountains, Indians rose up to fight the newcomers. "Pontiac's War" lasted from 1763 to 1764, with the British and colonists defeating the Indians.

The French and Indian War was a costly one on both sides. English and French colonists suffered at the hands of each other's armies and the Indians. Both sides committed atrocities. Various Indian tribes allied themselves with each country, and raided both French and English villages, killing soldiers and civilians alike. English officers would not listen to advice from colonial soldiers regarding ways to fight in the forest, and the colonists lost more men than necessary. The English borrowed large amounts of money, and by the end of the war, had a huge debt. To pay the war debt, the English Parliament and King George planned to levy a series of taxes on the colonists. They incorrectly believed Americans would pay the taxes out of gratitude for the British defeat of France.

King George III

Twenty-two-year-old George III became King of England in 1760, and within three years the British defeated the French in the French and Indian War. Immediately after the war, the king faced huge challenges. Indians, unhappy that the French lost, threatened the colonists, especially those who crossed the Appalachian Mountains. Great Britain owed 137 million pounds in debt, with 5 million pounds of annual interest. Also, on the continent where Great Britain invested so much in the war, an American people lived who believed in their right of representation, and who emerged from the war as experienced fighters. The young king's inability to deal with these new challenges led to his country's losing the colonies in the coming war.

Chapter 22

Land Regulation, Taxes, and Conflict

British land regulation and new taxes angered the Americans so much that it is not a far stretch to argue that they caused the American Revolution. Great Britain passed the Land Proclamation of 1763, along with a series of taxes. The Americans saw both of these actions as hostile, which ultimately led the colonists to unite and fight for their freedom.

Proclamation of 1763

For two main reasons, the British passed the Proclamation of 1763 which forbade colonists from traveling west of the Appalachian Mountains. Although the English won this land in the French and Indian War, they could not secure the safety of the colonists from the Indians, and in fact, the British had promised this land to the Indians. Great Britain also wanted to keep the colonists within its control, and it was easier to do this east of the mountain range. The colonists resented the Proclamation, and openly broke it.

One of these colonists was Daniel Boone (1734-1820), a brave explorer and adventurer who achieved legendary status as an American backwoodsman. Growing up on the colonial frontier, Boone learned how to be a hunter from the age of 12. As a young man, Boone went on months-long hunting expeditions, shooting bear and deer. He fought in the French and Indian War and was an officer during the Revolutionary War. After buying land from the Cherokee Indians in 1775, the Transylvania Company hired Boone to blaze a trail through the Appalachian Mountains, called the Wilderness Road. By 1800, over 200,000 people had used this road to travel into present-day Kentucky. Boone also established Boonesborough, Kentucky, the first colonial settlement west of the mountains. After the Revolutionary War, he led settlers inland and established new towns. Travelling into the Indian land of present-day Kentucky was dangerous. Indians were upset at outsiders encroaching upon their land, and felt that Indian land had to be defended against the white settlers. While leading a group of about 50 British colonists, Daniel Boone's son James and others were captured by the Indians, then tortured and killed. During his lifetime, Boone was captured by Indians multiple times.

TAXES AND THE AMERICAN RESPONSE

While westerners were upset with the British regulations regarding land, colonists along the Atlantic coast were angry about the Navigation Acts, a series of laws that limited Americans' sailing and trading rights. Americans were not allowed to trade directly with any country but Great Britain. Americans could not manufacture their own goods and could buy goods only from England. The Navigation Acts caused the politicians in the colonial assemblies, such as James Otis, Samuel Adams, and Patrick Henry, to forcefully assert the colonists' duty to start a revolution.

The Sugar Act of 1764 and the Stamp Act of 1765 also caused problems in the colonies. The Sugar Act was the first time the British taxed the colonies purely to raise money. The Stamp Act required all colonists to pay for a British stamp on every legal document. All marriage certificates, legal documents, newspapers, and even playing cards had to have a British stamp that cost a fee. The Stamp Act angered the colonists so much that colonists tried to break the law at every opportunity. An underground economy flourished, with playing cards and other paper items sold without the stamp.

Some Americans viewed the Sugar Act and the Stamp Act as a threat to their rights as Englishmen. Patrick Henry, a representative in the Virginia House of Burgesses, argued that the right to tax Virginians belonged solely to Virginia's representatives. He condemned the king and Parliament for their actions. Henry stated, "Caesar had his Brutus, Charles the First his Cromwell, and George the Third—" At this point, some representatives in the House of Burgesses were shocked and shouted, "Treason! Treason!" The punishment for treason was execution. Patrick Henry answered, "If this be treason, make the most of it." Eventually, Parliament repealed the Stamp Act.

After Great Britain repealed the Stamp Act, the king and Parliament moved quickly and passed other taxes on the Americans, and ordered British troops to occupy certain American cities. The Quartering Act of 1765 compelled colonists to house British soldiers and to pay for their food and housing. The Townshend Acts of 1767 were a series of laws that included taxes on many imported items such as tea, paper, lead, and glass. These items were not made in America and the colonists could only buy them from Great Britain.

In manifold response to these taxes, colonists voiced their opinions in their assemblies, wrote editorials in their newspapers, smuggled in items from other countries, boycotted British goods, and began to speak openly about the possibility of going to war against Great Britain. They also formed Committees of Correspondence, groups of leaders in each colony who wrote each other so that Americans knew what was happening in every part of the country. The equivalent today would be a type of social media where people could share common ideas.

THE BOSTON MASSACRE

By 1770, King George III placed British soldiers in Boston, both as a show of force and as a way to protect British tax collectors. Colonial leaders viewed these soldiers as an occupying force, and sought for ways to foment anger among all the colonists. The soldiers and the colonists came to violence. British soldiers were standing on patrol in the city when an American mob started throwing snowballs, then rocks, and yelling and screaming at the soldiers. To protect themselves, the British shot at the colonists, killing five and wounding six. Sam Adams labeled this incident "The Boston Massacre," Paul Revere engraved a picture of fierce soldiers firing into an unsuspecting crowd, and the picture was reprinted throughout the colonies. Though John Adams would represent the soldiers and defend them successfully in court, Americans believed the British to be violent oppressors.

The Boston Tea Party

One of the key events preceding the American Revolution, the Boston Tea Party (1773) captures the mood of the colonists, the impotence of the British, and the respect some Americans had for private property. Merchant ships brought tea into Boston Harbor. The Townshend Acts placed a tax on all imports, including tea. However, the British attempted to make this tax "easier to swallow" by making it so low that the cost of the tea on board the ship was lower than tea sold in Boston stores. Afraid Americans would buy this tea and thus pay the tax, a group of about 60 Bostonians, called the Sons of Liberty, dressed up as Indians, boarded the ships, and dumped the tea into the harbor. The incident outraged Benjamin Franklin because it injured the private company who owned the tea. Robert Murray, a New York merchant, offered to pay for the tea, but the British turned him down.

Intolerable Acts

To punish the colonists for the Boston Tea Party, Parliament passed the Coercive Acts, known as the "Intolerable Acts" in the colonies. Great Britain took away Massachusetts' self-government, closed the port of Boston, declared that all royal officials accused of crime be tried outside of the colonies, and forced colonists to house and pay for British soldiers with the passing of the Quartering Act of 1774. The British hoped that these laws would punish and isolate the wrongdoers in Boston, but instead, they caused many other colonists to go against Great Britain. The Intolerable Acts united the colonies like no other colonial argument could have.

CHAPTER 23

MOVING TOWARD WAR

FIRST CONTINENTAL CONGRESS

In 1774, delegates from twelve of the thirteen English colonies met for the first time ever in Philadelphia, Pennsylvania to discuss a course of action. The colonists wrote to King George III, petitioning him to rescind the Intolerable Acts. The Congress also declared a boycott of all British goods. This meant that the colonists would not buy anything made in Great Britain, or owned by a British company. The delegates also agreed that if the king did not rescind the Intolerable Acts, a second Continental Congress would convene in 1775.

Throughout the time before the American Revolution, delegates gave stirring speeches that resonated among Americans. At the First Continental Congress, Virginia representative Patrick Henry said, "The distinctions between Virginians and Pennsylvanians, New Yorkers, and New Englanders, are no more. I am not a Virginian, but an American." Later, in 1775, Henry stated, "Gentlemen may cry, 'Peace! Peace!' – but there is no peace! The war is actually begun. The next gale that sweeps from the north will bring to our ears the clash of resounding arms! Our brethren are already in the field. Is life so dear, or peace so sweet as to be purchased at the price of chains and slavery? Forbid it, Almighty God! I know not what course others may take; but as for me, give me liberty, or give me death!" James Otis, colonial leader in Massachusetts, spoke passionately about the right of each person to representation and to be secure in his home. His words, "taxation without representation," and "A man's house is his castle" still excite the imagination today.

THE IDEAS OF REVOLUTION

As written in *A Patriot's History of the United States,* two main streams of thought permeated the Americans' desire to risk their lives by going to war against Great Britain: Enlightenment ideas and Christianity. The theories of three thinkers of the Enlightenment, Thomas Hobbes, John Locke, and Baron Charles de Montesquieu, laid the groundwork for representative government. Adam Smith laid the philosophical foundation for the free market, an economic way of life that became America's engine of its first century and a half and transformed one of the world's weakest countries to the world's strongest.

Englishman Thomas Hobbes (1588-1679) wrote in his book *Leviathan* that man's life, without government, was "solitary, poor, nasty, brutish, and short." Government was created to protect life, and a monarch could have absolute power to do this. American colonists liked Hobbes' ideas that government was necessary to protect life. Englishman John Locke (1632-1704) wrote that government's job was to be limited to protecting life, liberty, and property. With a limited role, people would have maximum liberty. French author Montesquieu (1689-1755) wrote that to limit the abuse of power, government should be broken into three branches. Each branch would be responsible for some power, and each would make sure the other branches did not get too much control. Adam Smith (1723-1790) explained in The Wealth of Nations (1776) how the free market operates for the best of all people in capitalism. Capitalism was the system of economics in America throughout its first century.

Christianity was the second great philosophical thinking, or way of life and belief, that led to the American Revolution. Americans' reliance on a Christian God led them to believe it was their God-given right to have a representative government. John Adams, America's second president, wrote that the Revolution "connected, in one indissoluble bond, the principles of civil government with the principles of Christianity." John's cousin Sam Adams wrote that the Declaration "restored the Sovereign to Whom alone men ought to be obedient." Thomas Jefferson wrote in the Declaration of Independence, "…all men are created equal, that they are endowed by their Creator with certain unalienable Rights."

Most of the colonial leaders were strong Protestant Christians who believed in a personal God. We see this not only in their personal writings, but in the state constitutions with "Supreme Being," "great Creator," and "Preserver of the Universe" written throughout. It is true that Thomas Jefferson and Benjamin Franklin were perhaps deists, meaning that they believed in God more as a clock maker who created the world and let it run on its own. However, most colonial leaders believed as George Washington did. He wrote this prayer in 1752, "I humbly beseech Thee to be merciful to me in the free pardon of my sins for the sake of thy dear Son and only Savior Jesus Christ who came to call not the righteous, but sinners to repentance. Thou gavest Thy Son to die for me."

CHAPTER 24

THE BEGINNING OF THE AMERICAN REVOLUTION

NEW ENGLAND AND MIDDLE COLONIES PHASE OF THE WAR
LEXINGTON AND CONCORD: APRIL 19, 1775

The beginning of the war took place primarily in New England. The first fight of the war was not a traditional battle of two armies, but instead a skirmish, a fight that was not premeditated, between small opposing groups. Though small, the Lexington and Concord skirmish had monumental ramifications.

The skirmish at Lexington and Concord was fought because the British tried to stop the Americans from preparing for war. In 1774, American leaders at the Continental Congress in Philadelphia petitioned King George III and Parliament to restore their rights. When the king and Parliament refused and continued to hold the people of Boston under martial law, the Americans decided to mobilize for war. Colonists established illegal, revolutionary governments, collected taxes to fund militias and even funerals for soldiers, and established arsenals, which are warehouses for guns and ammunition. Americans were already well-armed, with each family owning several guns. However, men in villages now trained as soldiers. Town leaders chose and financially supported some soldiers, called minutemen, to be prepared to fight within a minute's notice.

General Gage, the commander of the British army in Boston, wanted to surprise the colonists. He ordered Major Pitcairn to march 1,000 soldiers 20 miles to Concord to destroy colonial ammunition and to arrest Samuel Adams and John Hancock. Gage did not want a fight, but wanted take weapons from the Americans so they could not fight. However, Americans in Boston learned of this plan and spoiled the surprise. On the night of April 18, 1775, a Bostonian set two lanterns in the belfry tower of the Old North Church, thus signaling to three riders, Dr. Samuel Prescott, William Dawes and Paul

Revere, that the British would go to Concord initially by a sea route.

The three riders set off from Boston to Concord, warning the colonists, "The Regulars are coming! The Regulars are coming!" The "Regulars" were the professional British soldiers. The three successfully alerted the colonists to arm themselves and meet the British.

In his Account of Midnight Ride to Lexington, (1775), Paul Revere wrote:

> *We set off for Concord, and were overtaken by a young gentleman named Prescot, who belonged to Concord, and was going home. When we had got about half way from Lexington to Concord, the other two stopped at a house to awake the men, I kept along.*
> *In an instant I saw four of them, who rode up to me with their pistols in their bands, said 'Stop. If you go an inch further, you are a dead man." Immediately Mr. Prescot came up. We attempted to get through them, but they kept before us, and swore if we did not turn in to that pasture, they would blow our brains out (they had placed themselves opposite to a pair of bars, and had taken the bars down). They forced us in. When we had got in, Mr. Prescot said "Put on!" He took to the left, I to the right.*
>
> *Just as I reached it, out started six officers, seized my bridle, put their pistols to my breast, ordered me to dismount, which I did.*

On the morning of April 19, 1775, the American Revolution started. About 700 British Regulars met less than 100 volunteer Americans assembled in Lexington, a village along the road to Concord. When the Regulars met the Americans, it was dark. Major Pitcairn ordered the Americans to disperse. They just stood there. Then, inexplicably, a shot rang out and the fighting started. The British killed eight and the Americans scattered. The British continued their march to Concord. In Concord, the British found the weapons and destroyed them. However, the Americans gathered there in far greater numbers and defeated a smaller group of the British at the Old

North Bridge. This victory energized the colonists.

The British were now twenty miles away from Boston, in the middle of hostile territory. For the rest of the day, the Regulars marched back to the city, drums beating, in formation, along a narrow road. During this march, Americans took aim at the soldiers, firing behind trees, stone walls, and fences, and then running away when any British soldier would chase them. British losses included 73 killed, 174 wounded, and 26 missing in action. American losses were 49 killed, 39 wounded, and 5 missing. Though a small victory, it was seen as a great triumph for the Americans over the strongest empire in the world.

SIEGE OF BOSTON

Thousands more Americans rushed to the aid of the Bostonians, setting up camp around the city, and trapping the British soldiers. Inside of Boston, Americans occupied Charlestown Peninsula, building fortifications on Breed's Hill and Bunker Hill. The British attacked, and the Americans fought bravely. Realizing their shortage of bullets and supplies, American Colonel William Prescott ordered his men to conserve their bullets. Reportedly, Israel Putnam said, "Don't one of you fire until you see the white of their eyes." The Americans lost the Battle of Bunker Hill, but shocked the British by killing and wounding many. Half of the British were either wounded or killed, and 12% of all British officers killed in the war died at this battle.

After the Battle of Bunker Hill, the American Congress realized that the war against Britain had begun, and made the crucial decision of the war: naming George Washington as Commander of the Continental Army. Washington immediately left Philadelphia for Boston, and took command of the 30,000 soldiers surrounding the city, and made plans to beat the British.

Boston bookseller and now army officer Henry Knox suggested to Washington that he order men to march about 300 miles north to capture Fort Ticonderoga, then take the cannons from the fort, and drag them back to

Boston. In January 1776, Knox arrived with the cannons. Washington positioned the cannons on Dorchester Heights overlooking Boston, and fired on the British. Realizing their hopeless position, the British fled by way of their navy.

The beginning of the American Revolution went amazingly well for the Americans. The Americans successfully beat the British at Lexington and Concord, fought extremely well at the Battle of Bunker Hill, and chased the British Army from Boston.

CHAPTER 25

THE DECLARATION OF INDEPENDENCE

On July 4, 1776, delegates at the Continental Congress approved the Declaration of Independence. This document is one of the most important in history and shows the incredible ideals and achievements of the American Founding Fathers. It is a work that does two things: it declares universal ideals for all people throughout the world, and it states that the United States of America is independent of Great Britain. Thomas Jefferson was the main author of the Declaration of Independence, and Benjamin Franklin and John Adams helped him edit and revise it. Jefferson took much of his writing from Englishman John Locke. Locke had written that government's job was to be limited to protecting life, liberty, and property. With a limited role, people would have maximum liberty. Jefferson and the Founding Fathers completely agreed with Locke.

In 1859, Abraham Lincoln wrote of the Declaration of Independence:
All honor to Jefferson—to the man who, in the concrete pressure of a struggle for national independence by a single people, had the coolness, forecast, and capacity to introduce into a merely revolutionary document, an abstract truth, applicable to all men and all times, and so to embalm it there, that to-day, and in all coming days, it shall be a rebuke and a stumbling block to the very harbingers of re-appearing tyranny and oppression.

Most people of the world do not have the liberties that Americans enjoy. Before the American Revolution, nobody did. Americans did not create the liberties won in the war against Great Britain, but they started the idea in the modern world that it is right for a people to be free. Since the Declaration of Independence was written, liberty has spread to all continents. The Declaration of Independence has become inspiring words not only for Americans, but for all people everywhere.

In the Declaration of Independence, Jefferson built on John Locke's ideas to write the ideals of the new nation, "We hold these truths to be self-evident, that all men are created equal." The notion that all men are created equal involves a number of ideas. The first is that there is one Creator of all men. Jefferson and the Founding Fathers believed in one God who created all things. The second idea in this statement is that the Creator gave all humans political equality. At birth, people were meant to have the same rights. One person was not intended to have more rights than another. In the British system, and in much of the world at the time, certain people in society had more rights than others. In the new United States of America, the ideal was for political equality.

At the time of the Declaration, there were slaves in America. However, Jefferson's writing on political equality was his vision of an ideal. It is important for a people to have an ideal to strive for. Eventually, the U.S.A. would rid itself of slavery, and black Americans would enjoy equal political rights.

Does political equality mean economic equality? Some people have falsely argued this. Having the same political rights does not mean that a people will be equal in every way. Jefferson did not write that all people will have the same amount of money, for example. This would require the end of freedom, as some people would have their property taken from them by force to redistribute to others.

Jefferson continued the Declaration by writing, "that they are endowed by their Creator with certain unalienable Rights; that among these are Life, Liberty, and the pursuit of Happiness." These are commonly referred to as "natural rights," as described by John Locke. They are natural because man has them through birth. No government gives man these rights. They are his naturally, from God. The right to life means that nobody is allowed to take a human life. Murder is against the law. Liberty means the right to political freedoms, such as the right of free speech and free press, and the right of religious freedom. The pursuit of happiness has commonly been understood to mean the right to own private property, but it also seems to imply more than this. In most of the world in the 1700s, people were not allowed to own property. Property was the right held only by the ruler, or by the ruling class. In the new country of the U.S.A., the American Founding Fathers firmly believed in every man's right to own land. This right allowed a person independence from the government, and the ability to establish a family and enjoy the fruits of one's labor.

The Declaration of Independence
IN CONGRESS, JULY 4, 1776
The unanimous Declaration of the thirteen united States of America
When in the Course of human events it becomes necessary for one people to dissolve the political bands which have connected them with another and to assume among the powers of the earth, the separate and equal station to which the Laws of Nature and of Nature's God entitle them, a decent respect to the opinions of mankind requires that they should declare the causes which impel them to the separation.

We hold these truths to be self-evident, that all men are created equal, that they are endowed by their Creator with certain unalienable Rights, that among these are Life, Liberty and the pursuit of Happiness. — That to secure these rights, Governments are instituted among Men, deriving their just powers from the consent of the governed, — That whenever any Form of Government becomes destructive of these ends, it is the Right of the People to alter or to abolish it, and to institute new Government, laying its foundation on such principles and organizing its powers in such form, as to them shall seem most likely to effect their Safety and Happiness. Prudence, indeed, will dictate that Governments long established should not be changed for light and transient causes; and accordingly all experience hath shewn that mankind are more disposed to suffer, while evils are sufferable than to right themselves by abolishing the forms to which they are accustomed. But when a long train of abuses and usurpations, pursuing invariably the same Object evinces a design to reduce them under absolute Despotism, it is their right, it is their duty, to throw off such Government, and to provide new Guards for their future security. — Such has been the patient sufferance of these Colonies; and such is now the necessity which constrains them to alter their former Systems of Government. The history of the present King of Great Britain is a history of repeated injuries and usurpations, all having in direct object the establishment of an absolute Tyranny over these States. To prove this, let Facts be submitted to a candid world.

He has refused his Assent to Laws, the most wholesome and necessary for the public good.

He has forbidden his Governors to pass Laws of immediate and pressing importance, unless suspended in their operation till his Assent should be obtained; and when so suspended, he has utterly neglected to attend to them.

He has refused to pass other Laws for the accommodation of large districts of people, unless those people would relinquish the right of Representation in the Legislature, a right inestimable to them and formidable to tyrants only.

He has called together legislative bodies at places unusual, uncomfortable, and distant from the depository of their Public Records, for the sole purpose of fatiguing them into compliance with his measures.

He has dissolved Representative Houses repeatedly, for opposing with manly firmness his invasions on the rights of the people.

He has refused for a long time, after such dissolutions, to cause others to be elected, whereby the Legislative Powers, incapable of Annihilation, have returned to the People at large for their exercise; the State remaining in the mean time exposed to all the dangers of invasion from without, and convulsions within.

He has endeavoured to prevent the population of these States; for that purpose obstructing the Laws for Naturalization of Foreigners; refusing to pass others to encourage their migrations hither, and raising the conditions of new Appropriations of Lands.

He has obstructed the Administration of Justice by refusing his Assent to Laws for establishing Judiciary Powers.

He has made Judges dependent on his Will alone for the tenure of their offices, and the amount and payment of their salaries.

He has erected a multitude of New Offices, and sent hither swarms of Officers to harass our people and eat out their substance.

He has kept among us, in times of peace, Standing Armies without the Consent of our legislatures.

He has affected to render the Military independent of and superior to the Civil Power.

He has combined with others to subject us to a jurisdiction foreign to our constitution, and unacknowledged by our laws; giving his Assent to their Acts of pretended Legislation:

For quartering large bodies of armed troops among us:

For protecting them, by a mock Trial from punishment for any Murders which they should commit on the Inhabitants of these States:

For cutting off our Trade with all parts of the world:

For imposing Taxes on us without our Consent:

For depriving us in many cases, of the benefit of Trial by Jury:

For transporting us beyond Seas to be tried for pretended offences:

For abolishing the free System of English Laws in a neighbouring Province, establishing therein an Arbitrary government, and enlarging its Boundaries so as to render it at once an example and fit instrument for introducing the same absolute rule into these Colonies

For taking away our Charters, abolishing our most valuable Laws and altering fundamentally the Forms of our Governments:

For suspending our own Legislatures, and declaring themselves invested with power to legislate for us in all cases whatsoever.

He has abdicated Government here, by declaring us out of his Protection and waging War against us.

He has plundered our seas, ravaged our coasts, burnt our towns, and destroyed the lives of our people.

He is at this time transporting large Armies of foreign Mercenaries to compleat the works of death, desolation, and tyranny, already begun with circumstances of Cruelty & Perfidy scarcely paralleled in the most barbarous ages, and totally unworthy the Head of a civilized nation.

He has constrained our fellow Citizens taken Captive on the high Seas to bear Arms against their Country, to become the executioners of their friends and Brethren, or to fall themselves by their Hands.

He has excited domestic insurrections amongst us, and has endeavoured to bring on the inhabitants of our frontiers, the merciless Indian Savages whose known rule of warfare, is an undistinguished destruction of all ages, sexes and conditions.

In every stage of these Oppressions We have Petitioned for Redress in the most humble terms: Our repeated Petitions have been answered only by repeated injury. A Prince, whose character is thus marked by every act which may define a Tyrant, is unfit to be the ruler of a free people.

Nor have We been wanting in attentions to our British brethren. We have warned them from time to time of attempts by their legislature to extend an unwarrantable jurisdiction over us. We have reminded them of the circumstances of our emigration and settlement here. We have appealed to their native justice and magnanimity, and we have conjured them by the ties of our common kindred to disavow these usurpations, which would inevitably interrupt our connections and correspondence. They too have been deaf to the voice of justice and of consanguinity. We must, therefore, acquiesce in the necessity, which denounces our Separation, and hold them, as we hold the rest of mankind, Enemies in War, in Peace Friends.

We, therefore, the Representatives of the united States of America, in General Congress, Assembled, appealing to the Supreme Judge of the world for the rectitude of our intentions, do, in the Name, and by Authority of the good People of these Colonies, solemnly publish and declare, That these united Colonies are, and of Right ought to be Free and Independent States, that they are Absolved from all Allegiance to the British Crown, and that all political connection between them and the State of Great Britain, is and ought to be totally dissolved; and that as Free and Independent States, they have full Power to levy War, conclude Peace, contract Alliances, establish Commerce, and to do all other Acts and Things which Independent States may of right do. — And for the support of this Declaration, with a firm reliance on the protection of Divine Providence, we mutually pledge to each other our Lives, our Fortunes, and our sacred Honor.

Chapter 26

Defeat, Surprise, and Survival

Just a month and a half after the signing of the Declaration of Independence, George Washington and the American Army were crushed at the Battle of Long Island. English brothers General Howe and Admiral Howe and over 35,000 British and Hessian (paid fighters from Hesse, Germany) soldiers and sailors nearly destroyed, captured, or scattered all of Washington's army of about 20,000. To the surprise of the British, Washington somehow escaped a seemingly hopeless situation with 3,000 American soldiers. Because of Washington's ability to lead his army away from capture, the British called him "the silver fox."

Though badly defeated, Washington kept the rest of his army together to fight another battle. Demoralized and in a dire situation, the soldiers of the Continental Army were in danger of disbanding and losing the war. Many soldiers had initially signed up to fight for 90 days, and it would not have been viewed as cowardice had they left. It was then that Washington ordered a daring attack that captured the imaginations of Americans then and today. On Christmas night, December 25, 1776, the Continental Army crossed the icy Delaware River and surprised 1,000 Hessian soldiers who had been celebrating Christmas, in part, by drinking large amounts of hard alcohol. The Americans captured the town of Trenton, and gained immeasurable amounts of enthusiasm and hope. Within the month, Washington led his soldiers in defeating the British, again, at the Battle of Princeton (1777), bravely riding his horse in between the British and American lines, calling out to his men, "Parade with us, my brave fellows…we will have them directly."

Perhaps the American low point of the war was the fall and winter of 1777-1778. The British defeated the Americans at the Battles of Brandywine and Germantown, and captured Philadelphia. The one bright spot for the Americans was that they won the Battle of Saratoga in the Mohawk Valley, defeating an army of 6,000 soldiers. While the British enjoyed the warmth of Philadelphia and New York City, the Americans spent the winter at Valley Forge, Pennsylvania, a cold and inadequately supplied fort. It was here that the American soldiers nearly lost all hope. They were poorly fed, lacked basic winter clothes, and felt abandoned by the American Congress and people.

One thing that kept up the hopes of Americans was the writings of Thomas Paine. A recent immigrant to America from England, Paine had failed in business and in two marriages. His second wife paid him to leave her. However, Paine wrote perhaps the most inspiring revolutionary essays in Common Sense, and later, The American Tract. Paine wrote, "These are the times that try men's souls. The summer soldier and the sunshine patriot will, in this crisis, shrink from the service of his country." American soldiers read from these books during their winter months.

But perhaps the most important factor in turning the tide of war at Valley Forge was the training of American farmers into a hardened, professional army. Foreign officers joined the Americans and trained the farmer volunteers. German Baron von Steuben, French nobleman Lafayette, Polish Count Pulaski and others voluntarily trained and fought alongside the Americans. After the winter of Valley Forge, the Continental Army was ready for battle.

Even though America had no official navy, American sailors captured great amounts of British supplies, destroyed ships, and conducted themselves in inspiring ways. In one battle, Captain John Paul Jones saw that his ship, the Bonhomme Richard, would soon be destroyed. He tied the Bonhomme Richard up with the British Serapis, won the battle, took over the Serapis, and let his own ship sink into the sea! Many say that John Paul Jones is the Father of the American Navy.

The French and the Southern Phase of the War

After the winter at Valley Forge, British General "Gentleman" Johnny Burgoyne moved to invade the Mohawk Valley in New York, but in his entourage were 400 women camp-followers, his mistress, his four-poster bed, fine china, best dress clothes, and other needless people and materials. Burgoyne met a tough and well-trained professional army. American General Horatio Gates had 12,000 militia and 5,000 regulars against Burgoyne's army of 6,000. In two engagements known as the Battle of Saratoga, the Americans completely destroyed or captured Burgoyne's army.

After the Americans won the Battle of Saratoga, French King Louis XVI was persuaded by American ambassador Benjamin Franklin that the Americans could win the war. The French joined the Americans in war against the British in February 1778, sending 30,000 muskets, 200 cannons, 25,000 uniforms, 1,000,000 pounds of powder (90% of total American powder), the French fleet, and a French army.

While the British defeated the Americans in most of the battles and occupied the major cities of New England and the Middle Colonies, they could not keep control of the countryside. The war was in a stalemate. The British decided they would focus their efforts in the South, where a greater percentage of Americans sided with Great Britain than in the North. In the South, however, Americans caused great harm to the British. "Swamp Fox" Francis Marion, Thomas Sumter, and Andrew Pickens led southern militia forces against the British. Nathaniel Greene led his soldiers in defeating the British at the Battle of Cowpens, South Carolina, and badly hurt the British at the Battle of Guilford Courthouse in North Carolina.

French Commander Rochambeau devised a trick that eventually led to the end of the war. Washington pretended to march soldiers to attack New York, but actually marched 5,000 soldiers to join with 5,000 French and met with Nathaniel Greene's army, who had outmaneuvered British General Lord Cornwallis. While these three armies surrounded Cornwallis at Yorktown, Virginia, the French fleet beat the English navy at sea, blocking the British escape. After some fighting, Cornwallis saw that his position was hopeless, and he surrendered on October 19, 1781. Americans captured 8,000 soldiers, 214 artillery pieces, thousands of muskets, and 24 transport ships. Even though the war continued for two more years, there were no other major engagements in North America, and the British lost interest in continuing to fight.

The first country in the modern era had won its independence from a colonial power and the world's first modern republic was established. To win the war, Washington realized that it was more important to never suffer such a defeat that he or all his men would be captured, and he outmaneuvered the British until France decided to send help. Between 40,000 and 60,000 American patriots gave their lives for their new country.

THE TREATY OF PARIS

In 1783, John Jay, Benjamin Franklin, and John Adams negotiated the Treaty of Paris with Great Britain. The United States of America won its independence, earned the right to navigate the Mississippi River, won fishing rights off Newfoundland, Canada, and won the rights to all the English holdings in North America south of Canada.

CHAPTER 27

THE ARTICLES OF CONFEDERATION, 1777-1789

From the very beginning, the United States of America was a country of laws, not of men. This means that all citizens had equal rights, and no one had any special privileges. It is very common throughout history, that when a country has a revolution, the reasons for the war are moral and just, but then, in the middle of the chaos, some group or person takes over and changes the meaning of the revolution so that it becomes violent and horrible. One amazing fact about the American Revolution is that the government of America remained stable, slow to change, and respectful of citizens and states throughout the war and through most of the following years. We can call this a political miracle.

The American Founding Fathers created the Articles of Confederation (a document) to organize the thirteen different colonies into one, united country. This new government of America consisted of 13 states that were in almost every way separate and independent countries. The Articles of Confederation united the colonies in one primary function: to wage war against Great Britain.

The reasons America went to war determined the first type of government it would have. Thomas Jefferson clearly wrote in the Declaration of Independence that all men had the right to life, liberty, and the pursuit of happiness, and that the role of government was to preserve these rights. King George III and Parliament had broken this agreement with the colonists. The British government had become too strong, and this was why Americans wanted a new form of government. Jefferson and the American leaders wanted this government to be strong enough to beat Great Britain, but so weak as to never encroach upon the liberties of individuals.

Under the Articles of Confederation, there was one Congress that made laws. Each state sent a delegation of two to seven people to Congress, and each state had one vote. Passing a law required 7 of 13 states to agree; passing a treaty or declaration of war needed 9 of 13 states. Unlike our government today, there was no president, and no judicial branch. The following liberties were guaranteed under the Articles: freedom of speech, habeas corpus, no cruel or unusual punishment, freedom of religion, freedom of the press, and the right to life, liberty, and private property. (Habeas corpus is a Latin term meaning "present the body." It means that authorities cannot arrest and detain someone without reason.)

To amend the Articles of Confederation required a unanimous vote. The Founding Fathers of the Revolutionary period did not want the Articles of Confederation changed, because they so greatly feared a strong government. Each of the states wanted to maintain its sovereignty.

Under the Articles of Confederation, not only did Americans succeed in winning the American Revolution, negotiating the Treaty of Paris, and beginning a peaceful transition from war into peace, they also settled the questions involving future states and the Indians.

The Congress of the Confederation decided that all of the territory west of the original 13 states to the Mississippi River would be organized into new states that had equal rights. This had never happened before in history. When Great Britain or France or Spain established colonies, the colonies always had less rights than the mother country. Colonies existed to serve the mother country. By granting the new states equal rights, it encouraged mass migration and settlement to the west.

The Land Ordinance of 1785, the Northwest Ordinance of 1787, and the Southwest Ordinance of 1789 provided for a peaceful, scientific and orderly settling of the western territories. The Ordinance of 1787 established that when 60,000 people inhabited a territory, they could write a state constitution and enter the country as a state, on equal footing with the original 13. The territories were divided into even squares forming thousands of townships, each containing 36 regions of 640 acres each. This division made it easy for land surveying, designing new towns, and granting land titles. The first law regarding land and rights passed by the U.S. Congress made slavery illegal. Slavery was outlawed in the Northwest Territories. In 1789, the Southwest Ordinance organized the Southern Territories in the same way, except that slavery was allowed.

Despite many accomplishments, the Articles of Confederation created a country that was so loosely united, that many argued that it needed to be changed. Congress had no power to tax, and could only ask the states for money. After the American Revolution, Congress disbanded the army, as there was no way of paying soldiers. There also was no president, and no judicial branch. This lack of an executive allowed for colonists to believe they had the right to rebel without repercussions.

Though the Articles of Confederation presented challenges, many Founding Fathers were happy with the structure of the new government. These Founding Fathers wanted the country to be loosely united, so that a strong federal government could never arise. These became known as the Anti-Federalists. The majority of historians think that most Americans leaned Anti-Federalist. The Founding Fathers who wanted to amend or replace the Articles of Confederation were called the Federalists.

Problems stemming from the Articles of Confederation nearly spelled the end of the young republic. Because Congress could not tax, it had problems paying soldiers. After the war, American officers discussed the possibility of taking action against the government. Only a personal plea from George Washington stopped the officers. In 1786, Daniel Shays, a retired officer from the Continental Army, organized an armed revolt of 4,000 farmers against tax and debt collectors in Massachusetts. Because there was no national army, a state militia was raised to put down this revolt. Washington saw this as a direct threat to the new country. A third danger came from foreign governments. Great Britain still had soldiers stationed in forts in the western territories. In addition, the British had high tariffs on American goods, but were able to make separate trade treaties with each state. America, with its weak central government, was not respected around the world.

UNIT V

The Constitution

Introduction

The American Founding Fathers were not all of one mind. Those who favored a stronger federal government were called the Federalists. Those who favored stronger state governments were called the Anti-Federalists. Because of the Federalists, America has a Constitution. Because of the Anti-Federalists, it also has a Bill of Rights that guarantees individual and states' rights. The arguments that took place during the writing of the Constitution are still part of the American political scene. Right at its beginning, Americans argued over the size of the American government.

During four summer months in 1787, Americans wrote what would become the world's oldest working Constitution. They met in a locked room, with windows nailed shut, in what has been described as "oppressively hot" weather. The founders met in secrecy, because they believed if some Americans knew what they were doing, their meeting would be disrupted or stopped. State legislatures appointed delegates, and 12 of the 13 states were represented. Rhode Island wanted none of it. Patrick Henry of Virginia refused to go and stated, "I smell a rat."

Chapter 28

The Making of the American Constitution

The American Founding Fathers were keenly aware of history, of governments and people of the past, and their goal was to take this knowledge and create a republican government for the American people that would last. The early chapters of this book focus on this history. The historical path towards the liberty established in the U.S. Constitution begins in the early civilizations of the Fertile Crescent, travels through the civilizations of Ancient Greece and the Roman Republic, and continues through medieval and early modern Europe, especially England. The religious beliefs and practices of Judaism and Christianity played significant roles in creating the world's first modern republic, and the virtues these religions teach and foster were key to establishing a strong and good republic.

The Declaration of Independence and the U.S. Constitution

The Constitution puts into effect the ideals of the Declaration of Independence, and the Founding Fathers saw these two documents as linked. When a territory applied as a new state, it had to first adopt the Declaration of Independence. The ideals of the Declaration of Independence, "all men are created equal," and, "they are endowed by a Creator with certain unalienable Rights, that among these are Life, Liberty, and the pursuit of Happiness," are codified in the structure of the Constitution. This belief in one God, and the rights of the individual were to always take precedence over any government.

The Convention

The Constitutional Convention was reportedly called not to create a new governing document, but to revise the Articles of Confederation. However, the delegates from Virginia, including James Madison, George Washington, and Governor Randolph, introduced a plan so radical that all realized that if they continued the discussions, the Articles would be abolished and a new form of government would be established.

Thomas Jefferson was in Paris during the convention, but after reading a list of names of those present declared the meeting to be "an assembly of demi-gods." Delegates included George Washington, James Madison, Benjamin Franklin, Alexander Hamilton, John Adams, Roger Sherman, and many other prominent Americans. At least one third had been officers in the Continental Army during the American Revolution. Franklin was the leading scientist, publisher, inventor, and abolitionist of his time period. George Washington was the man who had done more than any other to win America's independence.

Some patriots chose not to come, because they protested the idea that a stronger government was needed. Many Founding Fathers were against writing a constitution, including Richard Henry Lee, James Monroe, Patrick Henry, Aaron Burr, George Clinton, and Sam Adams. These men believed the convention would take away states' and individual rights and wrongly believed that by not attending the convention they would hurt the chances of a new government forming. These soon became the Anti-Federalists.

OPENING PROPOSAL: THE VIRGINIA PLAN
Probably no other delegate had thought and studied more about the weakness of the United States of America and its government than James Madison. He believed that the new country was going the way of most new countries—into complete disarray and disintegration. Great Britain did not respect America, and continued keeping soldiers on American soil in the West and attacking American merchant ships. State politicians argued with each other over taxes and tariffs. Also, there was no army to put down insurrections like Shay's Rebellion.

To counter what Madison saw as a country in decline, he began the Constitutional Convention by having Virginia Governor Randolph propose a completely new form of government. The Virginia Plan called for a government where power was separated into three branches, an executive, a legislative, and a judicial branch. The new plan called for a much stronger government than the Articles of Confederation created. With power divided into three branches, Madison believed tyranny would not rule the new country. Each branch would have its own work to do, and each branch would make sure the other two branches would not become too powerful. From this original plan delegates debated over key features, but basically, Madison had created the framework of the modern world's oldest living republic.

Key Debates

Forming a united and strong government from thirteen disparate states was nothing short of a political miracle. During the American Revolution, Commander George Washington saw the danger of the American forces not uniting for a single cause. In his attempt to bring the soldiers together, he attempted to have the fighters from different states swear a pledge to the United States of America. The soldiers would not do this, and instead insisted that they were fighting for each of their states. The soldiers of New York owed no allegiance to Virginia, and the soldiers from South Carolina did not necessarily like those from Connecticut. There was great distrust and even animosity between the citizens of the different states.

Big States versus Small States

The American Founding Fathers believed that the power to make law was the most important power of government. Because of this, the major arguments arose in the composition of Congress. In the Articles of Confederation, there was one Congress with each state having one vote. A bill did not become a law unless seven of thirteen states agreed. To the lesser-populated states, like Delaware with 54,000 people, this was highly favored. But for the densely-populated states, like Virginia with 735,000 people, this seemed unfair. How could the voice of 54,000 carry the same weight as that of 735,000?

The first proposal for a new government came from Virginia, a large state.

The Virginia Plan called for representation in Congress to be proportional. The heavily-populated states would have more representatives in Congress. Naturally, all of the delegates from the more populous states like Pennsylvania, Virginia, and Massachusetts liked this plan.

Delegates from the smaller states proposed their own plan, called the New Jersey Plan, or the Paterson Plan named after William Paterson. In the New Jersey Plan, representation in Congress would be by state. Each state would receive one vote. Naturally, less populous states like Delaware, New Jersey, and Georgia favored this.

To break this impasse, Roger Sherman of Connecticut proposed a compromise, which came to be known as the Great Compromise. This plan called for Congress to be composed of two houses: a Senate and a House of Representatives. In the Senate, each state would be equal, but in the House of Representatives, representation would be proportionate to the population of the state. For a bill to become a law, both the Senate and the House of Representatives had to approve the bill. The Great Compromise satisfied the delegates from the small states and the large states. The small states had their Senate and the large states had their House of Representatives.

DEBATES OVER SLAVERY

A second great debate of the Constitutional Convention was over slavery. A great many northern and some southern delegates opposed slavery, and slavery had already been banned in the Northwest Territories. However, enough southern delegates made it clear that if slavery were to be banned by the Constitution, then the southern states would never ratify the new governing document. It was clear at the convention that slavery was a contentious issue, and some Founding Fathers could foresee that this problem could result in war. But, in order for the county to be united, slavery had to remain an issue that each state decided.

One aspect of the slavery issue revolved around how slaves would be accounted for in determining representation in the House of Representatives, where the states with greater population received more representatives. A state also received the same number of electors as representatives to elect the president. In determining proportional representation, the question arose, "Will slaves be counted?" Northern delegates thought that since slaves could not vote, they should not receive representation and southern states should only receive representation based on the white population. Again, the southern delegates threatened to oppose the Constitution unless slaves counted for some representation. Delegates decided on the 3/5 compromise. This meant that every slave would count as 3/5 of a person. For example, 100 slaves would count as 60 people. So, since Virginia had 442,117 whites and 292,627 slaves in 1790, Virginia would receive as many representatives that 442,117 whites plus 60% of slaves (175,576) would account for. While this seems completely crazy to a modern American, without this compromise, the Constitution would not have been ratified. Also, without this compromise, the great Thomas Jefferson would not have won the presidency, as the southern states favored him over Adams, a northerner.

A third debate over slavery involved the international slave trade. Northerners wanted to end importing slaves from abroad, and southerners wanted to continue it. Delegates agreed on yet another compromise. In 20 years, if Congress wanted, it could end slave importation. Within those 20 years, slave importation would continue. Eventually, Congress did end the importation of slaves, but the domestic slave trade continued until the end of the Civil War.

Debate over Individual and States' Rights

The greatest challenge of the framers was to create a government strong enough to secure life, liberty, and the right to own private property for Americans, yet make sure the government would never become too strong that it could take away the rights of Americans and states.

What the government can do is specifically written in the Constitution. Congress' powers, for example, are found in Article I, section 8, clauses 1-18. The Founding Fathers thought Congress did not have power in any area that was not listed. However, over time, Congress has stretched its powers to include almost everything that was once considered state powers. For example, the U.S. government now decides issues involving health and education, even though these powers are not specifically listed in the Constitution. Because of the expanding powers of the federal government, many Americans think that states and individuals have less liberty than Americans enjoyed in 1790.

CHAPTER 29

PRINCIPLES OF THE CONSTITUTION

There are basic principles found in the Constitution. These include:
1. Men Are Not Angels
2. Limited Government
3. Federalism
4. Republicanism
5. Separation of Powers
6. Checks and Balances
7. Individual Rights
8. Sovereignty of the People

MEN ARE NOT ANGELS

James Madison wrote in Federalist Paper number 51, "If men were angels, no government would be necessary." The Founding Fathers created the oldest living constitutional republic with the belief that people are not perfect, and in fact individuals naturally strive for power over others. The challenge in building a strong government is to give it enough power to govern, but to restrain it so it will control itself. This principle is perhaps the most important in understanding the Constitution.

LIMITED GOVERNMENT

The American Founding Fathers created a government that was limited in power. They believed that it was more important for Americans to enjoy liberty than for their government to do everything. Americans remembered how British King George III and Parliament wanted to control the colonists, so they made sure that the new Constitution would never create a government that was too strong. The structure and function of the U.S. government was designed so that Americans would have maximum liberty and the government would be small.

Federalism

Federalism is the idea that there are various state governments and one federal government, each having its own spheres of power. The founders created this system for a few reasons. At the beginning of the United States of America, 13 different and separate colonies agreed to join to fight for independence from Great Britain. The colonies differed from each other in many ways, however. It was as if 13 different countries agreed to fight a common enemy. After joining to win its independence, each state wanted to maintain as much of its freedom as possible. Also, having various state governments is a defense against tyranny. It is more difficult for an autocrat to take over America, because America is a country with a wide variety of states, people, and ways of living. With different and strong state governments, it is much more challenging for a dictator to take control. For example, under the concept of federalism, the federal government makes decisions regarding war, but each state decides laws regarding education.

Republicanism

Republicanism is an ideology that favors a political system that is founded on the rule of law, the rights of individuals, and the idea that citizens choose leaders to make the law and govern. It emerged in the Greek city-states and the Roman Republic over 2,000 years ago, and did not exist again until Renaissance in Florence, Italy, early modern Britain and the founding of the United States of America.

Separation of Powers

The framers separated the powers of government into three branches to prevent tyranny. They were fearful that a person or small group might try to establish a monarchy or dictatorship, and thus each branch has separate powers.

Legislative Branch: Powers of the legislative branch are specifically written in Article I, section 8. Congress' main power is to make law. However, the laws of the legislative branch are not allowed to suppress the rights of individuals and states, as written in the Bill of Rights.

The Founding Fathers held that the legislative branch had the most important powers in the government—the powers to make law and declare war. To further limit this branch from abusing these powers, the framers created it with the most people. It is more challenging to get many people to agree on something than just a few people. Today, there are 535 Congressmen. It is hard to get all of them to do anything! This was exactly the intention of the Founding Fathers. The fewer laws Congress makes, the more liberty Americans have.

Executive Branch: Powers of the executive branch are stated in Article II of the Constitution. One of the main powers of the President is to be the Commander-in-Chief. This means that once Congress declares war, it is up to the President how to wage war. The President is not supposed to wage war without the consent of Congress.

Judicial Branch: Powers of the judicial branch are found in Article III of the Constitution, and in various decisions of the Supreme Court. The judicial branch is limited by the fact that it can only make decisions on court cases it hears. Justices and judges are not allowed to create a law from their discussions or from their feelings, but must respond directly to individual cases that are presented. The highest court in the land is the Supreme Court.

CHECKS AND BALANCES

Checks and balances is the concept that the three branches have powers that are specifically designed to counter the power of the other branches. These powers "check" the other branches and keep a "balance" of power.

The legislative branch (Congress) has powers that check the executive and judicial branches. Against the President, Congress can reject presidential appointments and reject treaties that the President negotiated. It can also override a presidential veto. A veto is when the President rejects a bill Congress passed. To override the veto, Congress can pass the bill with a 2/3 margin, and the bill becomes law. Congress can also impeach and remove the President. To impeach the President, the House of Representatives accuses the President of a crime. After a President is impeached, the Senate holds a trial, and can remove the President with a 2/3 majority vote. Against the judicial branch, Congress can impeach and remove judges, and it can reject presidential appointments.

The executive branch (President) has powers that check the legislative and judicial branches. The President can veto (reject) bills from Congress. The President appoints (chooses) justices and federal judges of the judicial branch, with Senate approval. The President can pardon criminals.

The judicial branch has powers that check the legislative and executive branches. Its main power, judicial review, is not part of the written Constitution. As explained in a later chapter, Supreme Court justices gave themselves this power! The judicial branch can declare laws of Congress and acts of the President unconstitutional. To declare a law unconstitutional means to declare the law void, not valid.

Chapter 30

Individual Rights

The Founding Fathers envisioned a country where individuals would live in liberty and have much responsibility. At our country's founding and for the next 100 years, the federal government did not directly influence the daily life of Americans. There was no welfare assistance for those without work. There was no government aid for someone who became ill and had no money to pay a doctor. The poor and needy relied on family members, friends, or the church to help out, not the government. Because of these limits on the U.S. government, Americans were some of the most independent-minded, capable, and charitable people in the world. Forced to do things on their own and freed from an outside government telling them what to do, the United States changed from one of the smallest and weakest countries, to the strongest and one of the richest in the world by the end of World War I, only 142 years after its founding. The modern world has no other similar example.

The individual rights of Americans are ensured by the Bill of Rights

Bill of Rights: The Bill of Rights contains ten basic rights of individuals and states, and specifically denies the federal government the right to make laws against these rights. The following are the Bill of Rights amendments paraphrased.

> **1. First Amendment:** This guarantees the right to free speech, freedom of the press, religious freedom, and the right to assemble. The founders were very concerned with freedom of political speech, meaning the right to campaign or financially support the candidate of one's choice without limitation. They wanted to make sure that government would never become so strong that it would limit Americans' abilities to participate in politics. Regarding freedom of religion,

the founders wanted to make sure the government would not enforce a state religion, however, at the same time, they wanted Americans to never be limited in their practice of religious worship. All leaders of the American republic invoked God during official speeches and addresses, and nearly all believed that religion was necessary for a successful republic. The idea of "separation of church and state" did not exist until the 1900s.

2. Second Amendment: The right to bear arms. This right was meant to ensure Americans had the right to own guns and to have state militias that could be a counterweight to the country's army.

3. Third Amendment: Citizens cannot be forced to house and feed soldiers. This amendment was written to make sure what King George III decreed for the colonists would never again happen.

4. Fourth Amendment: No unreasonable searches and seizures.

5. Fifth Amendment: People cannot be forced to testify against themselves in court.

6. Sixth Amendment: Citizens have the right to a speedy and public trial.

7. Seventh Amendment: Citizens have the right to a jury trial in certain cases.

8. Eighth Amendment: The federal government cannot impose excessive bail, fines, or cruel and unusual punishment.

9. Ninth Amendment: Rights not listed in the Constitution are retained by the people. This means that just because a right may not be written in the Constitution does not mean that a person does not have that right.

10. Tenth Amendment: All power not specifically given to the federal government in the Constitution is retained by the people or the states.

Historians Michael Allen and Larry Schweikart write that it is good to see the Bill of Rights as a "Bill of Limitations" on the federal government. These ten amendments make clear that the federal government does not have the power to infringe on the personal liberties of individual Americans, no matter the reason.

Popular Sovereignty

Popular sovereignty is the principle that only the consent of the people creates and sustains a state and federal government. The people are the ones in charge of the government. American elected officials are, in effect, the employees of the American people. Politicians have no special rights over others, and American voters can kick out officials during elections. The people give political power to politicians and the people can take it away.

UNIT VI

ERA OF THE FOUNDING FATHERS, 1787-1825

INTRODUCTION

In a new life, the most important years are the first few. Scientists report that the first three years of a person's life are most significant, and it is essential that an infant receives love, care, affection, and mental stimulation from birth to age three. For a new country, the first few years are the most important, as well. A new country has many challenges. Its government must be respected by its own citizens and by foreign governments. A new country is usually militarily weak and its institutions are new and untested. The United States of America had another challenge that no other new country had had in nearly two thousand years – it was a representative democracy. For the first time since the Roman Republic, citizens could vote for their own leaders.

From 1787 to 1825, America was led by the Founding Fathers. These men fought the British, established the American Constitution, and worked in the first few years of the new American government. Many have said that America's Founding Fathers were both the most intelligent and the most honorable men in the world.

The Era of the Founding Fathers is full of firsts:
1. The establishment of a representative government with a written constitution
2. The first modern republic in the world
3. The first peaceful exchange of power between opposing political parties in the modern world
4. The world's first all-volunteer military force since the ancient times
5. The first time new states received the same rights as the original states
6. The first time a slave and a woman voted (Lewis and Clark Expedition)

7. The expansion of representative democracy in North and South America
8. The first modern state where most education took place in the home
9. The first country in the modern world whose economy operated primarily under capitalist ideas
10. The first country where nobility was outlawed

This list could go on. The point is, the Founding Fathers established such strong institutions and traditions of representative democracy and capitalism that they propelled the United States of America from one of the world's weaker countries to the world's strongest and freest by the mid- to late 1800s. Much of what the Founding Fathers established exists today in America, and is emulated throughout the world's republics.

One great failure of the American Founding Fathers involved slavery. Though slavery was a moral evil, and though many Americans opposed it at the founding of the country, many other Americans favored slavery and its expansion. Slavery was incompatible with the country's ideal as expressed in the Declaration of Independence, "all men are created equal." Slave owners argued that slaves were private property, and therefore the government could not grant slaves their freedom. The failure to solve the problem of slavery eventually led to the U.S. Civil War, 1861-1865.

Chapter 31

Ratification of the Constitution

After the Founding Fathers wrote the Constitution in 1787, nine out of thirteen states had to approve, or ratify, the new governing document for it to become the law of the land. Nine is the number of states that James Madison and the Federalists decided, and it was a rather controversial decision. Under the Articles of Confederation, nine was the number of states needed to pass treaties and declare war, however, thirteen was the number of states needed to amend the Constitution. The new Constitution completely abolished the Articles of Confederation. In this light, the whole ratification process of the Constitution was illegal under the Articles of Confederation. However, there was no mechanism in place to stop the process of ratifying the Constitution.

Very quickly, two main groups or parties emerged: the Federalists and the Anti-Federalists. The Federalists favored the Constitution and the creation of a strong, federal government. The Anti-Federalists favored strong states and feared a strong, federal government. The ideas and arguments of these two sides dominated the ratification process, and they remain with us today. If an American can understand the main arguments of these two factions, or parties, then he can understand our political party system.

The Federalists

John Jay, Alexander Hamilton, and James Madison wrote a series of essays called The Federalist Papers which explained the reasons Americans should approve the new Constitution:
- America needed a strong, central government with a president to handle emergencies, such as wars.
- Separation of powers would provide security that not one person or group of people would act tyrannical.
- A large republic was needed to control passions (factions) of local populations.

If a group of people in one region of the country wanted something that would hurtothers, the rest of the country would make sure this small group would not dominate.
- A vigorous, centralized republic was best for the economy. One supreme law for the whole country would make it easier for businesses.
- The states would remain strong and in charge of most governmental activities.
- Americans would remain religious, and this added security would be another safeguard against despotism.

THE ANTI-FEDERALISTS

Patrick Henry, George Mason, George Clinton, Sam Adams, James Monroe, Aaron Burr, and Thomas Jefferson were prominent Anti-Federalists who questioned the wisdom of ratifying the U.S. Constitution. Thomas Jefferson was in France during the Constitutional Convention and wrote that he would support the document only if it had a Bill of Rights. Here are the main arguments of the Anti-Federalists:
- The Constitution created a central government that was so strong it would take away individual Americans' and states' rights.
- The U.S.A. just defeated Great Britain because their central government was too strong. Why create another strong central government?
- The Constitution had no Bill of Rights to guarantee the federal government would not take away rights of the state and of the individual.
- The president had no term limits.
- The judiciary branch could become too strong, creating its own powers.

LEGACY OF THE ANTI-FEDERALISTS

The arguments of the Federalists won the debate, the Constitution was ratified, and it became the law in 1789. However, the ideas and arguments of the

Anti-Federalists have greatly influenced America throughout its history. To begin with, the framers agreed that once the Constitution became the law of the land, a Bill of Rights would be added. Also, many states have term limits for politicians, and, over 150 years later, Americans decided to forbid a president from serving more than two terms by passing the 22nd Amendment. One important question the Federalists and the Anti-Federalists give us today is this: How strong or weak should the federal government be in relation to the states and individuals? How a person answers this question determines a great deal about the person's political philosophy.

THE BILL OF RIGHTS (1791)

The American Founding Fathers studied many examples of bills of rights, including the Magna Carta (1215), the English Bill of Rights (1689), and each state's bill of rights. James Madison, called "Father of the Constitution" because he was the primary author, wrote a 12-amendment Bill of Rights, and 10 of these were passed as the Constitution's first 10 amendments (see the previous chapter).

Chapter 32

The American People

In 1776, the newest country on Earth began. Inconsequential at first, the United States of America would become a world superpower. It is worth noting what those first Americans were like, how they lived, and learn what their customs and beliefs were. Knowledge of this can help us understand how this country grew in numbers and in strength over the next two centuries.

A great majority of Americans were farmers who owned their own farms. This meant that each family owned its own business and carried all the responsibility for making enough money to eat, have clothes, have a home, and take care of family. On the farm, women and girls were in charge of making nearly all clothes that were worn and cooking all the food, in addition to helping with the farm work. Men and boys did farm labor and hunting. If the family members made poor business decisions or ran into bad luck, they lost their farm.

While each family was independent in numerous ways, most families lived in small communities that shared many things. Families held community get-togethers, built the town church together, decided local political issues, and hired a teacher together to educate their children a few months of the year. In many ways, each community was like its own country, with each family taking an active role in community affairs.

Most Americans were Protestant Christians who believed it was essential to read the Bible. This common knowledge of the Bible and similar understanding of morality helped Americans form communities and laws. Society functioned without an extensive police force or written laws, because most people shared the understanding of what was the correct thing to do, and there was no need for many law officers.

Americans reproduced in great numbers, and immigration to America kept a steadily-increasing pace throughout the first 150 years of the republic. More children meant more laborers for the farm, since at a very young age, by five or so, children were put to work to help out with the family business. In 1790, the U.S. population numbered under four million. By 1890, it had grown to 70 million. This is a growth of more than 1700%. In 1890, New York State had more people than all of America in 1790. In 1790, most Americans lived within 50 miles of the Atlantic Ocean. The Mississippi River was America's western boundary, but it seemed like the moon for the majority of Americans.

Travelling long distances was a horrible affair in the early republic, and because of this most Americans did not ever leave their state. The fastest means of travel in the early years was by sailboat, and the speed of this mode depended on the wind. On land, Americans travelled by walking, horseback, and stage wagons on poor roads. Travel from Boston to New York took six days. By car, this takes about 3 ½ hours today. People moved west by the Conestoga Wagon, a vehicle that could hold up to 6 tons (12,000 pounds) and weighed up to 1,800 pounds.

Schools were everywhere, but New England had more than the other colonies. Schools were financed by private funds. During the winter months, when it was impossible to work on the farm, private teachers lived with the family of one of the schoolchildren. Boys were taught to read and write and do arithmetic. Girls were taught how to read and write, but more academic work was demanded from boys, and girls were expected to master household work over schoolwork.

Colleges included Harvard, William and Mary, and Yale, and the primary purpose of these institutions was to train ministers. Women were not allowed to attend. In academic areas, America lagged behind Europe, but as a new country fighting for its survival, this was understandable. Americans were busy cutting down trees and building homes. Most literature concerned religion and politics. American artists such as John Copley, Benjamin West, and John Trumbull earned reputation as painters in Europe, but art was not a part of typical American life. One scientist was perhaps the most famous in the world—Benjamin Franklin. Franklin was an inventor, scientist, writer, publisher, and statesman. Nearly all know of his kite-flying experiment that proved lighting was electricity.

The average day for the early American revolved around the sunlight. With no electricity, no telephone, and no telegraph, Americans lived an existence very close to nature. Americans heated their homes with wood and cooked over fires. Lamps or candles lit homes. Oil from whale blubber fueled all of New England's lighting. Because of this limited lighting, Americans went to bed early and got up early. This, along with their Christian religious beliefs and the small government, led Americans to be very industrious people.

One-seventh of Americans were slaves in the early 1800s. Very few of them lived in the North, and none in Massachusetts or Maine. Almost all slaves were in Virginia, Maryland, and North and South Carolina. In less than 20 years, practically all the northern states banned slavery and Americans stopped importing slaves.

CHAPTER 33

FATHER OF THE COUNTRY

Historical events have patterns that seem to repeat, regardless of the country, time, or place. Regarding revolutions, it is the same. At first, rebels rise against the government and claim to want to throw out a strong, overpowering regime. A strong man emerges, who completely takes over, and refuses to relinquish power. A fight for leadership ensues. There is bloodshed, and the initial reason the rebels had in overthrowing the strong government disappears. Yet, the American Revolution shattered this pattern, in large part because of the character and actions of George Washington.

In 1789, the year Washington became president, America was faced with many challenges. The country was small, divided by state loyalties, attacked by outside countries, threatened by neighbors in all directions, and in huge debt from a war it had just barely won. On top of this, the United States of America was trying out a form of government that had not existed on Earth for 1,800 years, and trying this out in a large territory. The actions of Washington and his advisors established the framework that the new country could build on over the next centuries.

FEDERALISTS AND REPUBLICANS

From the very beginning, American leaders were split into two main factions, or ways of thinking, about how government should look and operate. Though Washington disliked political parties and tried to dissuade others from beginning or joining them, they naturally formed during his two terms. One party became known as the Federalists, and the other party the Republicans.

(Please note: The names of the political parties of the 1790s are not the same names as the political parties of our times. Though the Republicans of the 1790s called themselves Republicans, some modern textbook authors call this party the "Democratic-Republicans" or the "Jeffersonian Republicans." This book will

call the parties the name they called themselves, the "Republicans" and the "Federalists.")

The main point these two sides argued about was the size and power of the federal government. The Federalists wanted a stronger central government, and the Republicans wanted the states to be stronger. The Federalists thought that with a stronger central (or federal) government, the country would be better defended from foreign enemies, stronger to build a growing economy, and it would be united. The Republicans thought that with stronger states, Americans would enjoy more liberty, be free to live as they choose, and build healthy families and strong farms. The graph below roughly shows which Americans were attracted to the two parties and what the parties stood for. Of course, there were exceptions.

REPUBLICANS	**FEDERALISTS**
Jefferson, Monroe	Hamilton, J. Adams, Washington, Marshall
Farmers	Merchants and Bankers
Planters	Tradesmen
Agrarian	Cosmopolitan
South and West	Northeast
Smaller Government	Expansive Government
Weak Army and Navy	Strong Army and Navy
Bill of Rights	Distrusted Common People
Tended to be Pro-Slavery	Tended to be Anti-Slavery
Pro-Expansion	Reluctant Expansionists

Even though these parties formed during Washington's presidency, they were nothing like they are today. Partly because of George Washington, politicians attempted to work together, were united in their defeat of the British, and were interested in seeing the new American republic succeed. However, by 1796, many of the Founding Fathers were not on speaking terms.

Banking Policy

Washington established the cabinet in one of his first actions. The cabinet is a group of advisers to the president, who are also in charge of executive departments. Cabinet members are in charge of foreign affairs (Secretary of State), war (Secretary of War), finance (Secretary of the Treasury), and other executive departments. The president is in charge of his cabinet members, and he directs them. The cabinet is not a part of the Constitution, but Washington created it, and every president since has had a cabinet. Through the cabinet, the president enacts his policies. Washington chose the best leaders of the day, and he chose men who had strongly differing views. Though Washington knew he was not the smartest man in the room, he was not afraid to choose more intelligent men to advise him. This display of courage and humility helped the new country in many ways.

Two of Washington's cabinet members – Alexander Hamilton and Thomas Jefferson – became bitter political enemies. Hamilton wanted a strong, central government that would support a thriving business class, and he wanted the wealthy to become directly involved with the success of the republic. Jefferson wanted a weak central government so that the states and individuals would be free to enjoy their lives. In many ways, George Washington favored the ideas of Alexander Hamilton.

Hamilton proposed policies that Washington promoted, and these became the economic policies of the young United States of America. As a result, America quickly became a respected country in the world and Americans benefitted greatly. Hamilton proposed the following actions taken by the American government:

1. The federal government assumed all debt of the states and paid it back 100%. During the American Revolution, states borrowed money from Americans and from foreign countries, and it was difficult for the states to pay it back. Because the federal government paid back the debt, America gained respect from foreign countries, and American merchants could do business overseas. It also placed the states under the power of the federal government.

2. The federal government sold bonds to Americans and gave wealthier Americans a stake in the success of the new country. When someone buys a government bond, the government promises to pay back the bond at a later date with more money. People who bought American bonds gave the country a loan, and the health of the country determined if it could pay back the bonds. Selling bonds to Americans made wealthy Americans work toward strengthening the country because they wanted to have their bonds paid off.

3. In selling bonds, the federal government created a new national debt. Alexander Hamilton stated, "A national debt is a national blessing."

4. The federal government established a National Bank that was 80% owned by private investors. This bank printed money, helped the government pay its workers, and was a source of credit for people and businesses to borrow money.

Hamilton's banking policies upset James Madison and Thomas Jefferson. They did not like that wealthy Americans were given favors by the federal government, and they thought it was unfair to states that had paid their debt, that now everyone had to pay the debt of other states. James Madison eventually moved to the party of Jefferson, the Republicans.

WHISKEY REBELLION

In 1794, George Washington led a force of 13,000 soldiers to crush a rebellion by western Pennsylvania farmers, known as the Whiskey Rebellion. West of the Appalachian Mountains, many farmers brought their produce to market by putting crops onto boats and sailing down the Mississippi River. Alternately, they used poor roads. Because corn is heavy and challenging to transport, and because Americans liked to drink whiskey, farmers turned the corn into whiskey and sold the liquor. The federal government placed a tax on whiskey, which was proposed by Hamilton to help pay the Revolutionary war debt. The farmers protested, created an army, and threatened to kill tax collectors and government officials.

The Whiskey Rebellion greatly disturbed President Washington. He said, "If the laws are to be trampled upon with impunity, then there is an end put, with one stroke, to republican government." Washington's soldiers quelled the protesters without a fight and the leaders were tried and sentenced to death, then Washington pardoned and freed the leaders. Jefferson despised the use of American soldiers against Americans.

Foreign Policy

The foreign policy problems of the young United States of America were existential. This means that each of the challenges to the United States from abroad threatened the existence of the young and relatively weak country.

In 1789, the French Revolution began, and for the next 26 years, America faced a resulting gauntlet of challenges that nearly destroyed our country. Revolutionary Frenchmen wanted to overthrow their king, establish a republic, and spread revolution to all of Europe. They wanted Americans to help them. But the French Revolution became bloody, destructive, and dangerous. When Napoleon Bonaparte took over France in 1799, he wanted to take over Europe, and wanted the U.S. to help in defeating Great Britain. But Great Britain wanted America's help in defeating the French.

President George Washington wanted America to stay clear of the French Revolution and France's war against the British. He issued the Proclamation of Neutrality in 1793. Washington's proclamation made it clear that America would not support Great Britain or France in the war. However, the British attacked American ships at sea, and impressed, or kidnapped, American sailors and forced them to work on British naval ships for years. Also, the French attacked American ships at sea, destroying American property and killing American sailors. Washington knew America was not strong enough to go to war against France or against Great Britain.

Thomas Jefferson strenuously objected to the Proclamation of Neutrality because he wanted the U.S.A. to support France. As the Secretary of State, Jefferson thought that he was unable to support the policies of President Washington, and thus he resigned.

In 1795, Washington succeeded in having Great Britain and Spain agree to treaties that opened the West for settlement and made the seas safer for Americans. In Jay's Treaty, the British promised to evacuate its forts on American soil in the West and to allow American ships safe passage on the seas. In Pinckney's Treaty, Spain promised to allow Americans safe travel on the Mississippi River. Many Americans were angry at Washington because they wanted their country to go to war against Great Britain, but he thought America was too weak to win another war, and he wanted to give America time to get stronger.

In the West, Americans streamed in over the Appalachian Mountains into the Northwest Territory. Indians who had lived there for centuries, like the Miami, the Shawnee, and the Delaware, fought back. After American forces lost under General Saint Claire, Washington ordered General "Mad" Anthony Wayne to fight, and he defeated the Indians at the Battle of Fallen Timbers. Wayne negotiated a treaty with the Indians, the Treaty of Greenville (1795), which allowed for safe immigration of Americans to the West.

In northern Africa, a number of Muslim countries believed that their religion gave them authority to capture and enslave Americans. In 1786, Thomas Jefferson and John Adams asked Tripoli's ambassador Sidi Haji Abdrahaman why Tripoli was making war on nations who had not harmed it. The ambassador replied, "It was written in their Koran, that all nations which had not acknowledged the Prophet [Muhammad] were sinners, whom it was the right and duty of the faithful to plunder and enslave; and that every mussulman [Muslim] who was slain in this warfare was sure to go to paradise." The young America was not yet strong enough to challenge the Muslims, thus America paid $1 million every year for approximately 15 years as "tribute" so the Muslim nations of Africa would not attack Americans at sea. Washington created a navy in 1794, but it remained weak its first few years.

Farewell Address

George Washington refused to serve a third term as president. He thought that it was time for a new leader, and for him to go back to his farm at Mount Vernon. This act of relinquishing power did not have a modern equivalent. In addition, Washington did this twice, in 1783 and 1798. Nowhere on Earth in the modern world was there another person who had done this. Washington had done all he could to establish a republic where changes of power would happen peacefully.

In his farewell address, Washington stated that Americans required God and religion to maintain a republic. He wrote, "Religion and morality are indispensable supports." He also wrote that Americans would not have "security for property, for reputation, for life if the sense of religious obligation desert the oaths" of officeholders. Without religion, Washington believed that the best possible plan of government, the Constitution, would not stand.

Regarding foreign policy, Washington urged the young country to be patient as it gained in strength and military prowess before entering into a war. He wrote, "Twenty years peace with such an increase of population and resources as we have a right to expect; added to our remote situation from the jarring powers, will in all probability enable us in a just cause to bid defiance to any power on earth." Incredibly, it appears that Washington was correct. In about 20 years, America joined the world as one of the stronger powers to be reckoned with.

Legacy of George Washington

Congress commissioned Henry "Light Horse Harry" Lee to write a eulogy for Washington after he died in 1799. Lee captured what all thought of Washington, and how Washington would be perceived by future historians. He wrote, "First in war, first in peace, and first in the hearts of his countrymen, he was second to none in the humble and endearing scenes of private life; pious, just, humane, temperate and sincere; uniform, dignified and commanding, his example was as edifying to all around him, as were the effects of that example lasting."

Washington is the measure by which all presidents are judged. The cabinet system he created still exists in its basic form and purpose. At the country's founding and for many years afterward, Americans demanded high moral principles from their presidents. All presidents, except one, have served a maximum of two terms. Americans generally want their presidents to be unifiers and not engage in rough and tumble politics. The United States of America was both lucky and blessed to have as their first president the greatest man in the world.

CHAPTER 34

PRESIDENCY OF JOHN ADAMS
(1797-1801)

Because of George Washington, the change of power from Washington to Adams was peaceful, and America accomplished what had not happened in the world since the Roman Republic: a people elected a leader, and the one in power stepped down. John Adams, a Federalist, continued the domestic policies of Alexander Hamilton and George Washington by favoring a more powerful central government.

QUASI WAR

During the presidency of John Adams, Great Britain and France continued attacking Americans at sea, with the English impressing, or kidnapping, American sailors and forcing them to work on British ships for years. (A small number of those impressed were actually British deserters). Many in America wanted war against our European enemies, but Adams thought we were not yet ready, and did everything in his powers to keep the U.S.A. out of war. Still, unofficial war happened, called the "Quasi War." Quasi means real, or apparent. American ships were attacked by the French and the British, and because America was a young country, it had a rather weak army and navy, so it did not defend itself.

DOMESTIC POLICY

Because of the Quasi War, Americans were outraged at the French and English, and Federalists believed that the French were sending spies to America. Under these circumstances, Congress passed and President Adams signed the Alien and Sedition Acts in 1798. Under the Alien and Sedition Acts:

1. Naturalization increased from four to fourteen years. This meant that an immigrant had to live in the U.S.A. for fourteen years before he could apply for citizenship.

2. The president could deport aliens for any reason.
3. Judges could imprison those who spoke or wrote against the government, or against the Federalists. The law was written in such a way that the judges had much power in how they determined if someone should be locked up.

Analysis of Adams' Presidency

John Adams accomplished two main things during his presidency: he made sure Federalist ideas would rule the judiciary for much of the next century, and he kept the country out of war with Great Britain and France. Through Adam's appointments of many judges, he established that the federal government was supreme, and that the economic principles of capitalism and open markets would be the American system for the 1800s. The Alien and Sedition Acts were a violation of the very Constitution Adams had pledged to uphold, and it is partly because of his support of these unconstitutional laws that Adams lost the presidential election of 1800.

Election of 1800

Many historians consider the election of 1800 to be the most important election in the history of the world. It was the first time in the history of the United States of America (and it had not happened in the world for over 1,700 years) that power changed from one party, or group, to another, without war. Republican Thomas Jefferson beat Federalist John Adams. Both sides were strongly critical of each other, and it is a sign of American exceptionalism that in our founding and for nearly 100 years afterward, power changed hands without war.

CHAPTER 35

THE SUPREME COURT, JUDICIAL REVIEW, AND CAPITALISM

In the early 1800s, most of the world's economies existed to serve the king. Subjects worked to enrich the ruler and were subject to the will of the king. In the United States of America, however, the Founding Fathers established an economic system that was based on liberty, with the unfortunate exception of slavery. A man worked not to enrich the ruler, but to benefit himself and his family, and in turn his community. This system is called capitalism and it is reliant on a government establishing fair rules of competition, protecting property rights, and letting individuals choose the winners and losers. The Supreme Court of the early 1800s was essential in establishing the national free market of America.

Chief Justice John Marshall wrote the decision that gave the Supreme Court its greatest power, Judicial Review. Judicial Review is the power to decide if a law is constitutional or unconstitutional. Judicial Review is not granted in the Constitution, but it became the law through the court case Marbury v. Madison (1803). To illustrate the concept of Judicial Review, suppose Congress and the president make a law stating that Joan is not allowed to go to church or teach her children her religion. Joan could hire lawyers and sue Congress and the president for breaking her First Amendment rights, which include the right to practice one's religion. In this court case, the Supreme Court could decide that the law is unconstitutional, and this would delete, or erase, the law. This is an example of Judicial Review.

Chief Justice Marshall not only wrote that the Supreme Court can determine if a federal law is unconstitutional in Marbury v. Madison, but he also wrote in another decision, Fletcher v. Peck (1811), that the Supreme Court has the power to review state laws and determine if they are unconstitutional. In

Dartmouth College v. Woodward (1819), the Supreme Court used the power of Judicial Review to establish capitalism, free enterprise, and open markets in America in the 1800s. The court ruled that a contract is inviolable, that a state or an entity cannot individually void a contract. These decisions established the primacy of law and contractual arrangements in society. In many countries of the world, the government changes the law or disregards contracts in order to serve itself. In those countries, it is difficult or impossible for businesses to thrive, because people cannot plan and do not have freedom. America's founders made a nation of laws, not men. Regardless of who is in charge, each person has to follow the law. These legal and economic policies enabled Americans to build an economy that provided one of the highest standards of living in the world by the end of the 1800s.

In another Supreme Court case, McCulloch v. Maryland (1819), the justices ruled that no state can tax a federal institution and that the Bank of the United States was constitutional. Chief Justice Marshall's court declared that a state cannot impose its will on the federal bank. The court also decided that Congress may establish a bank to help it do what is "necessary and proper," as stated in Article I, Section 8 of the Constitution, to fulfill its constitutional responsibilities. This decision made it clear that the federal government was supreme over the state governments.

In the case Cohens v. Virginia (1821), the Supreme Court ruled that it had judicial review over states' courts, as well. This decision ensured that a state court could not overrule the Supreme Court, and that the laws of the country would apply nationally. This made doing business in America easy to understand and consistent. A business could eventually grow to encompass large areas and serve millions of people, instead of being limited by laws from various states. This is called "interstate commerce."

In Gibbons v. Ogden (1824) and Charles River Bridge v. Warren Bridge (1837), the court established property rights in a free society, interstate trade open to all competitors, and declared a state cannot forbid a company to compete. The right of a person to own property and know it is safe from others, even the government, is key to a free society.

Capitalism, Free Enterprise, and Open Markets in America in the 1800s Except for Slaves

Capitalism is a set of principles and behavior of people based on the principles of individual and property rights. In a country where capitalism is practiced, citizens have maximum freedoms and responsibilities. Laws govern interactions between individuals and everyone is treated the same. The result of capitalism is the free market, a place where individuals can buy and sell items or services, as each person thinks is best. In capitalism, the government is small and acts as a referee, ensuring that no one cheats or violates property rights. Free enterprise and open markets describe a society where the government places few restrictions on individuals, companies, and trade.

In America, from its founding until about 1913, capitalism, free enterprise, and open markets described the economy of the country, except where related to slavery. The Founding Fathers established a limited government in creating the Constitution. This limited government placed only a minimum of restrictions on Americans. The Founding Fathers wanted to encourage an economy that was as far away from an all-controlling king and government as possible. Unfortunately, slavery was allowed to exist in the South, and because of this the South did not fully participate in these economic freedoms.

The Marshall Supreme Court reaffirmed capitalism as America's economic system in key court cases. As noted above, in Dartmouth College v. Woodward (1819), the Supreme Court affirmed that contracts had to be kept, and that a state government could not violate a contract. In Gibbons v. Ogden (1824), the court ruled that only the federal government could regulate interstate commerce. In other cases, the Supreme Court favored competition and developing private property.

The intention of the Founding Fathers was to create a society where individuals could pursue their interests and passions, and where a strong government, such as a king, could not dictate to others. The result was possibly the fastest rise to world power ever seen in history, the strongest economy, and one of the highest standards of living in the world. Capitalism was the main reason immigrants flooded to the U.S.A. throughout the 1800s. The Supreme Court rulings reaffirmed the intentions of the Founding Fathers and ensured that Americans enjoyed living in the most economically free country in the world, at least in its first century.

Chapter 36

Presidency of Thomas Jefferson
(1801-1809)

As the third president, Thomas Jefferson reduced governmental powers and debt, doubled the size of the country, oversaw the beginning of the Great Migration west, defeated West African pirates through military action, and weakened America's international standing with Europe's great powers. It was through his domestic policies, however, that Jefferson firmly established the United States of America as a free republic with peaceful elections and transition of power.

Republican Thomas Jefferson Beat Federalist John Adams

As the first president taking over from an opposing party, Jefferson united the country, forgave his political opponents, and governed as an average citizen. In his inaugural address, Jefferson stated, "[E]very difference of opinion is not a difference of principle. We have called by different names brethren of the same principle. We are all Republicans, we are all Federalists." Under Jefferson, the Alien and Sedition Acts expired, and the political rights of the First Amendment were reinstated. Jefferson rode to his inauguration on horseback, signifying he was an average man. Also, he shook hands instead of bowing, and this practice became commonplace in America.

The Great Migration West

Thomas Jefferson's policies encouraged the Great Migration. The Great Migration refers to the unprecedented movement of millions of people into the western part of the United States of America throughout the 1800s. The lure of cheap or free land, political liberties, and free markets in America enticed people from around the world to first move to America, and then migrate west across the Appalachian Mountains and throughout the rest of America to the Pacific Ocean. People of various backgrounds and nationalities decided as individuals or families to give up their homeland and start anew.

What began as an attempt to add one city, ended up as a purchase doubling the size of the United States of America. Thomas Jefferson wanted to secure a free and safe trade route for Americans living west of the Appalachian Mountains. In the West, farmers took their crops to market by travelling on the Mississippi River down to New Orleans. In New Orleans, farmers sold their crops, or loaded their crops onto ships and took them around Florida and up the Atlantic Coast to New York City or to another large trading center. From 1763 to 1801, Spain owned Louisiana. In 1801, Spain returned it to France. Jefferson feared the French would block Americans' access to this important city.

In the early 1800s, France was at war with nearly every major European power. Napoleon Bonaparte wanted to conquer Europe, and then perhaps the world, and he needed money. When Americans Livingstone and Monroe offered to buy New Orleans, Napoleon's minister Talleyrand responded, "What will you give for the whole?" Americans spent $15 million for Louisiana (about 3 cents an acre), an unbelievable deal that secured not only New Orleans for western farmers, but huge swaths of land for future Americans.

No one knew what the land was like in most of the Louisiana Territory. The thousands of Indians who lived there did not draw maps or write books, and the few backwoodsmen who may have ventured there did not keep any records. Some believed it was a vast desert, unsuitable for farming. To solve this mystery, Thomas Jefferson appointed his personal aide, U.S. Army Captain Meriwether Lewis. Lewis then appointed soldier William Clark to help him lead a force of 50 soldiers and boatmen to explore the new American land.

LEWIS AND CLARK EXPEDITION

The Lewis and Clark Expedition was a journey akin to traveling to Mars and back, and it was a complete success. The Americans did not know exactly what to expect, how long it would take, and what they would find. Along with exploring and mapping the new land, Lewis and Clark were tasked to find and log new animal and plant species, befriend the Indian tribes, explore trade possibilities, and find the Pacific Ocean. Leaving in May 1804, and returning in September 1806, the expedition opened up the West for rapid American settlement.

Many accomplishments of the Lewis and Clark Expedition were examples of American exceptionalism. The lone woman on the expedition, Sacagawea, became a key reason for the expedition's success. She and a black slave became the first woman and slave to vote in history. This military expedition fought no battles, but was aided by Indians who could have killed everyone. The Shoshone woman Sacagawea was one of two wives of Frenchman Charbonneau. Sacagawea guided the men through her native homeland, bravely saved important materials when the expedition's boats were overturned into rapids, and carried a pregnancy to birth. She named the baby Jean Baptiste.

The Lewis and Clark Expedition provided detailed maps of its journey, encouraged other explorers to go west, and opened up the West for hundreds of thousands to move and settle. It may be President Jefferson's greatest accomplishment.

THE BARBARY WAR (1801-1805)

Under President Jefferson, the United States of America started and won a war against countries in northern Africa on the Barbary Coast. This was the first time America attacked another country first, which is called a preemptive strike. The reason for the war goes back to the beginning of the United States of America. After America declared its independence from Great Britain, its ships did not enjoy the protection of the British Navy. Muslims from the Barbary Coast attacked Americans at sea, captured sailors, and made them slaves. The Muslim countries believed the religion of Islam gave them the right to enslave non-Muslims.

In 1786, an envoy from Tripoli demanded payment for the release of the Americans, and a yearly tribute to halt the attacks. America did not have the military at that time to challenge the Muslim countries, and could not pay for the release of all the hostages. However, for the next 15 years, America paid about $1 million per year to the Barbary Coast states to dissuade them from attacking American ships.

In 1801, Congress gave Thomas Jefferson authority to go to war. Jefferson informed all the Barbary States that the U.S.A. was at war against them. This bold action to attack the Muslim countries ended with huge success. In 1804, American Lieutenant Stephen Decatur snuck ashore in Tripoli with eight Marines and burned the Philadelphia, an American ship that the pirates had captured. Around this same time, William Eaton marched across the desert, invaded Tripoli, and forced the pirates to release American prisoners. This mission became part of the Marine Song ("From the halls of Montezuma to the shores of Tripoli").

Problems with Great Britain and France

Despite Jefferson's bold actions against the Barbary Pirates, he did not like the idea of a strong military, and he let America's army and navy shrink during his presidency. This had dire consequences for America's relations with Great Britain and France. In the early 1800s until 1812, Great Britain was at war against France in the Napoleonic Wars. Both countries wanted America to help its own side. When America did not aid either one, they both attacked America. Great Britain impressed (kidnapped) 10,000 Americans at sea, forcing them to be British sailors, and seized American ships. The French attacked American ships that were trading with Great Britain. Jefferson's navy had no big warships and could not respond.

Thomas Jefferson thought that the best way to handle the abuse from the two countries was to stop trading with both of them. Congress passed and he signed the Embargo Act of 1807. This act made it illegal for any American to trade with any country. The results were disastrous. The new law nearly destroyed shipping towns in New England and crushed American industry. Great Britain took over all of American shipping, and many American sailors chose to break the law by trading illegally.

Analysis of Jefferson's Presidency

The presidency of Thomas Jefferson ensured that America would become the dominant country on the continent, but he endangered the young country by not building up the military. He was instrumental in taking the new republic peacefully from the rule of the Federalists to the Republicans. He cut the size of government bureaucracy, budgets, and debt. He allowed the Alien and Sedition Acts to expire, and did not seek revenge on the previous Adams administration. Through his purchase of the Louisiana Territory and his commissioning the Lewis and Clark Expedition, Jefferson sparked the Great Migration west.

Jefferson's foreign policy actions were not completely good. His bold action in defeating the Muslim nations of North Africa gave notice to America's enemies that no piracy would be tolerated. However, Jefferson's insistence on a weak army and navy ensured that the major powers of the world, Great Britain and France, could exert their will against American interests with no repercussions. Jefferson's Embargo Act was a disaster to the American economy and to American shipping.

CHAPTER 37

PRESIDENCY OF JAMES MADISON
(1809-1817)

The major event and success of the Madison presidency was the War of 1812, nicknamed "The Second American Revolution." As a result of this war, the United States of America gained international respect, was never again militarily challenged by Great Britain, and defeated the Indians. James Madison, though initially a Federalist, had become a Jeffersonian Republican who embraced strong states. However, Madison demanded international respect for America from Great Britain, and used the military to assert it.

TRADE POLICY

James Madison and Congress reversed course regarding the Embargo Act of 1807. Jefferson's Embargo Act had made it illegal for America to trade with any country. This resulted in economic disaster. Congress repealed this with the Nonintercourse Act (1809) that made it legal to trade with everyone except France and Great Britain. This also completely failed, and Congress replaced it with Macon's Bill (1810) which reduced trade restrictions on Americans. For most of the 1800s, this was the U.S. policy. It resulted in a growing American economy.

FOREIGN POLICY AND THE WAR OF 1812

The Madison Presidency was extremely active in foreign policy, fighting wars against the Indians, the Muslims of North Africa, and against Great Britain. In each of these conflicts, Madison was successful. After Madison, the United States of America was never again considered one of the weaker powers of the world, and it was able to expand.

From 1812 to 1815, the United States of America fought the Second Barbary War. The Muslim countries of North Africa again challenged America's right to sail the Mediterranean Sea without being attacked and enslaved. In this second war, the Americans won convincingly, and the Barbary Pirates nearly ceased being a danger to the American desire to sail. Fighting against those who held Americans hostage instead of negotiating with kidnappers became the American policy for the next centuries.

The War of 1812 is called the Second American Revolution because America fought Great Britain again to ensure the British would respect America's right to exist as an independent country. Although the Treaty of Ghent (1815), which ended the war, signified no great change in American territory, the United States achieved great success in the war and it was a pivotal moment in American history.

Though the war started in 1812, its causes can be traced to the days just after America won the American Revolution in 1783. Since then, Great Britain had treated America with disregard, impressing (kidnapping) her sailors at sea, occupying forts on American soil, damaging her trade with other countries, and arming and encouraging Indians on the frontier to kill Americans. In 1811, Americans suspected the British were arming and organizing the Indians under Tecumseh and his brother "The Prophet." After General William Henry Harrison defeated the Indians at the Battle of Tippecanoe (1811) in the West, James Madison and Congress decided the country was ready and able to defeat the British in war again.

For the Americans, the War of 1812 brought both horrible defeats and great victories against the British and the Indians. On land, the British succeeded in repelling the American invasion of Canada three times and successfully attacked and burned Washington, D.C. President James Madison and his wife Dolley barely escaped capture, and saved important documents from the White House before it burned.

The greatest land battles for the Americans were against the Indians in the South and at the Battle of New Orleans. General Andrew Jackson led an assortment of soldiers, Indians, and former slaves to defeat the Creek Indians in Alabama. Jackson also defeated the British at the Battle of New Orleans. The Americans killed over 2,000 British soldiers and lost only 21 men. From then on, Jackson was referred to as the "Hero of New Orleans."

The Battle of New Orleans occurred two weeks after the peace treaty ending the war was signed. Because the treaty was signed in Europe, it took almost two months for the news to cross the Atlantic Ocean by ship.

At sea, Americans won naval battles that shook the world. In the 1700s and early 1800s, Great Britain had the strongest navy in the world, yet American privateers took or destroyed a great number of British ships. Commodore Perry directed American sailors to build a fleet near Lake Erie, launched the fleet, and defeated the British at the Battle of Lake Erie (1813). Perry said, "We have met the enemy, and they are ours—two ships, two bridges, one schooner, and one sloop." Americans on the U.S.S. Constitution sank or captured the British ships Guerriere and Java.

RESULTS OF THE WAR OF 1812

The War of 1812 was a resounding success for the young country. Though the original reason for the war (British attacking Americans at sea) was not part of the Treaty of Ghent, the British never again posed a threat to America at sea or on land. The British also withdrew from their forts on American soil. In 1813, Great Britain defeated France, and this led to Great Britain no longer feeling the need to attack American ships. However, the victory gave Americans much hope and confidence. In addition, during the war, the Americans defeated the Indians in the Ohio Valley, Alabama, Mississippi, and Florida. From this time on, east of the Mississippi River, Indians no longer posed a threat to the country.

As a result of the War of 1812, the Federalist Party died. Federalists wanted American shipping and trade more strongly protected, and thought that the War of 1812 was disastrous to America's maritime interests. Federalists opposed the war, and some even tried to separate from the country. When the U.S.A. won the war, many Americans viewed the Federalists as traitors. Thus, when the war ended, the Federalist Party ceased to exist.

CHAPTER 38

THE ERA OF GOOD FEELINGS

In 1817, a Boston journalist wrote that the United States of America had entered into an "Era of Good Feelings." The young country had just defeated the greatest naval and military power in the world for the second time in 35 years. Americans had destroyed the Indian threat throughout the country up to the Mississippi River. In addition, abundant land seemed to guarantee citizens and their posterity farms and families for centuries. The Federalist Party had died out, and three successive presidents, Thomas Jefferson, James Madison and James Monroe, called themselves Republicans. The country was united and expanding west.

The American Founding Fathers and their immediate successors established a country of laws, where individuals could strive to follow their dreams, work hard, and develop technology and better ways of achieving their goals. For the most part, government intervention in society did not exist, and Americans enjoyed the fruits of their labors. This hands-off policy, also known as laissez-faire, allowed Americans to create and manufacture some of the world's best instruments, tools, and goods. Moreover, the standard of living rose rapidly and attracted immigrants from around the world.

During the twenty years following the War of 1812, however, American leaders failed to resolve the greatest problem of their time: the existence and spread of slavery. While many of America's laws reflected the immorality of slavery, the country was divided, North and South, free and slave. Jefferson's purchase of the Louisiana Territory presented the greatest blessing and challenge for the new nation: would slavery expand, stay, or recede? Instead of resolving this problem to the satisfaction of both sides, political leaders sought tactics and strategies to achieve and maintain power, expand government, and ignore the issue of slavery.

PRESIDENCY OF JAMES MONROE (1817-1825)

James Monroe was the country's fifth president and the last of the American

Founding Fathers. A man of great integrity, he had very little party feeling and was extremely popular. He dressed traditionally and was the last president to wear his hair in a ponytail. He favored a weak presidency and was a strict constructionist. This meant he thought the federal government had power to do only what was explicitly written in the Constitution. In 1820, he was reelected without any opposing candidate.

Monroe favored public works, but only if they were related to national defense. The federal government created and improved coastal forts. However, Monroe opposed the government spending money on roads, canals or other projects if they were not strictly related to defense, because the Constitution does not give the federal government this power. In 1822, Monroe vetoed a bill that would have authorized federal funds to improve the Cumberland Road. Monroe claimed, "it is with deep regret, approving as I do the policy, that I am compelled to object to its passage and to return the bill to the House of Representatives, in which it originated, under a conviction that Congress does not possess the power under the Constitution to pass such a law."

James Monroe achieved great success in the area of foreign policy. He settled the U.S.-Canadian border dispute through a treaty with Great Britain. In Georgia, his administration ordered General Andrew Jackson to defeat the Seminole Indians, who had been raiding settlers and then escaping into Spanish Florida. Jackson illegally invaded Florida, conquered the Indians, and found two British agents, then tried, convicted, and hung them as spies. Spain was thus forced to sell Florida to the U.S. for $5 million in the Adams-Onis Treaty of 1819. However, Monroe is best known for the Monroe Doctrine.

The Monroe Doctrine of 1820 forbids any European power from meddling in the affairs of North and South American countries in return for America staying out of European affairs. In the early 1800s, Spanish colonial power in the Americas was weakening, and France appeared to want to take Spain's possessions. Great Britain secretly assured America it would use its navy to defend the Americas.

Chapter 39

American Spirit and Industry in the Free North

The economic system the Founding Fathers created allowed individuals from all economic levels to aspire to and achieve incredible success. Slavery is the exception to this. Because of slavery, most technological advancements did not originate from the slave culture in the South. The South's medieval society stunted technological and economic advancement. However, the North was another story. At no other time in the history of man did one society invent and develop so many new ways of doing things that benefitted the general public. Many of America's most successful industrialists were born in this time period, including Andrew Carnegie (1835), J.P. Morgan (1837), John D. Rockefeller (1839), and Levi Strauss (1829). Most came from the poorest of backgrounds and were able to capitalize on the American environment of small government supported by laws that did not favor one group over another. The South, with its slave culture, repressed Americans who were hard-working, thrifty, and creative. Inventors created new products which improved the lives of all humans, and businessmen created systems that brought these products to average people, but the great majority of inventors in America were from the North.

The 1800s in America was a time of amazing technological breakthrough and rapid economic expansion. Because of the abundant land, scarce labor, and limited government, Americans were always thinking of better ways to work in agriculture. Along with new inventions, Americans also devised processes to make the inventions profitable and available to the average person. The following is just a small list of Americans who invented or developed processes in the 1800s that made many of life's tasks easier and thus raised the standard of living for the average American:

    1. James Oliver developed and advanced the iron plow and established a powerful company.

2. Charles Lane mass produced the iron plow.
3. Gail Borden invented an amphibious vehicle and developed the process to make condensed milk.
4. John Deere developed the finest farm machinery in the world and mass produced his machines.
5. Cyrus McCormick invented the McCormick reaper to harvest grain and hay. McCormick first created his reaper in 1834. Soon after, he was producing 4,000 a year. With his reaper, an American did the work of a European reaper in 1/3 the time.
6. Eli Whitney invented the cotton gin. One person operating this engine did the work of 40 men. This invention increased the bales of cotton produced in the South from 200,000 in 1800 to over 4,000,000 in 1860. Unfortunately, this invention also made slavery more profitable. Eli Whitney also developed the "American System of Manufacturing," creating products with interchangeable parts that could be assembled and repaired quickly.
7. Samuel Slater built the first textile mill in the U.S.A.
8. Francis Cabot Lowell established textile production factories with living arrangements for workers.
9. Robert Fulton made the steamboat commercially successful, and operated a transportation system on the Hudson River.
10. Samuel F. B. Morse invented the electric telegraph and Morse Code in 1835. Messages could be sent by wire over great distances.

These inventors and business developers were either northerners or westerners, or they moved to the North to further their business interests.

The first half of the 1800s was known as the "Canal Era." Perhaps the most important canal built in America was the Erie Canal. The Erie Canal connected the Great Lakes area to the Hudson River, which emptied into the Atlantic Ocean via New York City. This canal was 40 feet wide, 4 feet deep, and 363 miles long. The Erie Canal made New York City the business capital of the country.

CHAPTER 40

Railroads, the Post Office, and the Politicization of News

The Canal Era ended as the steam-powered railroad, an English invention, became the fastest means of travel on land, and completely changed transportation. Americans greatly expanded railroad use through private companies. The first successful commercial railroad in America was the Baltimore to Ohio line in 1828. By 1840, railroad tracks in the United States had reached almost three thousand miles; by 1850, more than nine thousand miles; by 1860, over thirty thousand miles. The American Railway Association created four time zones in America in 1883 to standardize train arrivals and departures. It is telling that a private organization was responsible for standardizing the time in America. American developments in the railroad industry include the parlor car, sleeping car, hotel car, dining car, street tramway, and elevated railways for rapid travel in cities.

Thus, Americans experienced a transportation revolution in the 1800s. Cornelius Vanderbilt used steam technology and business intelligence to cut travel time and travel cost. Vanderbilt's transportation company competed against state-sponsored businesses and won. He cut the New York to California travel cost from $600 to $100 per person and travel time by 50%. Railroads also opened up the interior of America for settlement.

Small government allowed for maximum freedom in business. Compared to today, there were practically no regulations on business, and there was absolutely no welfare state that required high taxes. By 1840, the U.S.A. equaled or surpassed Great Britain in ship building, iron manufacturing, publishing, and textile manufacturing.

The explosion of American technology, entrepreneurial spirit, and expansion west had some unintended consequences. The U.S. Post Office became one of the most powerful governmental organizations. Newspapers became politicized and widespread. Lastly, politicians who held office (incumbents) gained great advantage through the policy of "franking."

Franking is from the Latin word francus meaning free, and in Britain, certain kinds of mail could be sent free and the senders enjoyed the "franking privilege." In 1775, Congress gave its members the right of franking. Franking allows politicians the right to send mail without postage. The original idea was to allow for an inexpensive way to get news out. However, soon after the country was founded, American politicians used franking privileges to send political information to help them get reelected. It became extremely challenging to win an election against an incumbent.

Federal politicians favored the growth of post offices, because it allowed for more franking. The federal government paid for an explosion of post offices throughout the country and subsidized the cost of sending mail and newspapers. Because of this, printing and mailing newspapers became cheap. Also, political parties founded newspapers for the sole purpose of maintaining power by controlling information. In 1800, 2 million newspapers were sent through the mail. In 1840, 140 million newspapers were sent. Americans grew accustomed to reading current events and not books. They believed they were intelligent and up-to-date, however, the lack of books made them less classically-trained than their counterparts in Europe.

The United States Post Office became a political powerhouse. The Postmaster controlled more than 8,700 jobs in 1840. The highest echelons of the Post Office consisted of political appointees who enjoyed high salaries. The government wanted to protect the Post Office so much that it pursued criminal action against any companies that tried to deliver the mail. Post offices could not be established in towns unless there was easy transportation access. Railroads made the growth of post offices possible.

Much later, during 19 months of 1860-1861, Americans sent mail across the

West by way of the Pony Express. In the Pony Express, riders rode horses at breakneck speed. Every ten miles, riders would exchange horses at stations. This mail service was approximately 1,900 miles long, with 184 stations along the way. It started at St. Joseph, Missouri and ended in Sacramento, California. Mail then was taken by steamboat down the Sacramento River to San Francisco. Each rider rode about 75 miles per day. The railroad and telegraph took away the need for the Pony Express.

Chapter 41

The Missouri Compromise

The United States of America grew at a rapid pace from 1789 to 1821, and especially from 1816 to 1821. During the first 32 years of its existence, the new country added 9 states, but in those last 5 years, 6 states were added. Unheard of throughout the world, the new states entered on an equal footing with the original 13 states. The new states were not treated as colonies, and the "new" Americans had the same rights as the "original" Americans. This is one more example of American exceptionalism.

With the rapid expansion of the country, the question and problem of slavery became more acute. By the early 1800s, all the Northern states had abolished slavery, viewing it as an evil. How, then, could slavery be good in one part of the country and evil in another? Americans understood this moral inconsistency, but it appears that America's leaders hoped the problem would somehow go away on its own.

The slavery problem came to a crisis in 1819 with the application of Missouri to become a state. Missouri's application to statehood was the first from the Louisiana Territory. In 1819, the United States had 11 free states and 11 slave states. The North controlled the House of Representatives because more people lived in the North. However, the Senate was evenly divided. This meant that for a bill to become a law, it had to be agreeable to politicians representing both slave owners and non-slave owners. If Missouri came in as a slave state, those from the free states feared that those from the slave states would make laws that favored slavery. If Missouri came in as a free state, those from the slave states feared that Congress would make slavery illegal.

There is a story that we do not know is true, but it illustrates how grave a threat was the entrance of Missouri into the United States. It is believed that

Thomas Jefferson had a nightmare about Missouri, and woke up in a sweat as if he heard a "fire bell in the night." Americans saw that the problem of slavery in the United States was a terrible dilemma. How would new states from areas in the Louisiana Territory be added? Would they be free or slave? There was no easy answer.

To resolve this issue, Northern and Southern politicians developed the Missouri Compromise. Led by Henry Clay, politicians from the North and South agreed to the following:
1. Missouri entered as a slave state.
2. Maine entered as a free state.
3. Throughout the rest of the Louisiana Territory, there would be no slavery north of the parallel 36°30', except within Missouri.

The Missouri Compromise resolved the slavery issue temporarily. Thomas Jefferson saw it as a "reprieve only, not a final solution." From 1820 to 1860, as America expanded west and grew into an economic powerhouse, the problem of slavery grew until Americans finally resolved it in the catastrophic Civil War.

UNIT VII

THE BEGINNING OF BIG GOVERNMENT, 1825-1836

INTRODUCTION

The slavery crisis temporarily resolved by the Missouri Compromise also led to the creation of the modern Democratic Party. Martin Van Buren, a New York politician, feared that the problems caused by slavery might lead to a catastrophe, such as a civil war. To prevent this, he devised a national political strategy to elect politicians as leaders of a party whose goal was to maintain power and restrain discussion of slavery. When James Monroe, the last Founding Father to serve as president, left office, the Jeffersonian Republican Party splintered. Van Buren's organization stepped into this political vacuum.

While in New York, Van Buren had created a powerful political machine. Known as the Bucktail Republicans, it was a party based on patronage. Patronage means the power to reward others for their support, either with jobs or money or other benefits. Van Buren perfected this process, also called the spoils system. The Bucktail Republicans owned newspapers, controlled political news, and above all, worked to maintain power. Helping the Bucktail Republicans would eventually result in some sort of reward, such as a better job.

The new national organization Van Buren founded is the modern Democratic Party. Democrats favored suffrage (the right to vote) for all white men as a weapon against privileged classes and as a way to appeal to the masses. Up to that point, only white property-owners could vote. Van Buren wanted election campaigns to debate topics not related to slavery, with the idea that the country would never become torn over that issue, but would stay focused on other concerns. The Democrats appeared to represent the common man;

however, Van Buren's party favored the continuation of slavery while banning any discussion of this crucial topic. This contradiction – favoring the common white man but keeping millions of blacks in slavery – eventually led to the rise of Abraham Lincoln and the Republicans in the 1860 election. However, for decades, Southerners and some Northerners could vote for the Democrats, regardless of their differing opinions on slavery.

The growth of government came with limits to liberty. The more the federal government does, the less liberty individuals have. Under Presidents Jackson and Van Buren, the rights of American Indians were taken away. According to law, various American Indians had rights to reside in territories they had negotiated with the American government. Jackson and Van Buren, however, ignored these treaties, ignored a Supreme Court decision, and broke the Constitution by using federal troops on state territory to forcefully remove native peoples.

Chapter 42

The Election of 1824 and the Presidency of John Quincy Adams

After James Monroe, the Republican Party was in crisis. There was no clear leader to fill in after the last Founding Father. Four candidates competed for president, all calling themselves Republicans. John Quincy Adams, the son of the second president and fiercely anti-slavery, was perhaps the most qualified, but was cold and unfriendly. Adams said of himself, "I am a man of reserved, cold, austere, and forbidding manners." A second presidential candidate was Speaker of the House Henry Clay. A third candidate was strongly pro-slavery Georgian William Crawford. Andrew Jackson, the Hero of New Orleans, ran by not taking a stand on key issues and portraying himself as a commoner, though he was a wealthy attorney with a large plantation.

The election results were split, with no candidate winning a majority of popular or electoral votes. Popular vote means how many people voted for a particular person. Electoral vote refers to votes that each state has to award to a particular candidate. To become the U.S. President, a candidate has to win over 50% of the electoral vote. In the election of 1824, this is how the votes were split:

1824 Election	Popular Vote	Electoral Vote	Percentage
Andrew Jackson	151,271	99	41.4%
John Quincy Adams	113,122	84	30.9%
Henry Clay	47,531	37	13%
William Crawford	40,856	41	11.2%

According to the Constitution, when no candidate wins over 50% of the electoral vote, members of the House of Representatives vote for the president. At the time, Henry Clay was Speaker of the House. The Speaker of the House is one of the most powerful politicians in the American government. The House chose John Quincy Adams as the sixth president, and this decision both doomed Adams' presidency and increased Andrew Jackson's national appeal.

Because Jackson had won more votes than any other candidate but lost the election, he felt cheated. After Adams became president, he appointed Henry Clay as Secretary of State, arguably the second or third most powerful position in government. This appointment made it appear that Clay had a crooked deal with Adams. Jackson and his supporters called it the "Corrupt Bargain," and though there is no evidence Adams and Clay had made a deal, most Americans believed they had.

Adams was unable to accomplish anything of merit, and he made no friends or allies during his tenure. He even lectured Congress not to be led by the will of the voters. He was the last president to call himself a Republican until Abraham Lincoln. Never again would there be single-party rule in America. Jackson's allies became increasingly vitriolic in their attacks against Adams. Van Buren and Jackson teamed up, and Andrew Jackson ran as a Democrat in the presidential election of 1828.

CHAPTER 43

THE AGE OF JACKSON
(1828-1835)

Andrew Jackson is the first president from the modern Democratic Party. Jackson was a famous president whose supporters idolized him and called him the spokesman for the "Common Man." However, Jackson was a flawed individual and his legacy is controversial. Was he for states' rights? Was he for greater national power? Was he a hero or a villain? These are all legitimate debate questions. Throughout his presidency, Jackson worked toward two things: attaining more power for himself and the Democratic Party, and making America stronger in his eyes. If there was a policy that benefitted Jackson, he supported and fought for it, whether it was unconstitutional or if it strengthened or weakened national or state power. If Jackson thought that stepping on the rights of Native Americans would make America stronger, he did it. If Jackson thought he needed to break state and federal law and violate the Constitution to strengthen his party, himself, or the country, he did it. It appeared to many people that he championed the common man and states' rights, but his actions often went against this appearance.

1828 ELECTION

The election of 1828 was hot and vitriolic, full of personal political attacks and void of any discussion of the slavery problem. This was exactly what Martin Van Buren wanted. Jackson and his supporters argued that Adams' "Corrupt Bargain" made him unfit for the presidency, and even that Adams had given an American servant girl to the Russian Czar. Adams and his supporters claimed that Jackson was a whiskey-drinking, dueling, slave-abusing idiot who was married to an adulteress. Jackson crushed Adams in the popular vote, winning an astounding 56%, and capturing 178 electoral votes to Adams' 83.

INAUGURATION

One immediate result of the election was tragic. Rachel Jackson, Andrew's wife, had suffered chest pains during the election, and on December 22, she died. Jackson held the Adams' campaign guilty because they had attacked Rachel's character, claiming she had been married to two men at the same time. Jackson said, "I can and do forgive all my enemies. But those vile wretches who have slandered her must look to God for mercy."

A second immediate result of the election was an embarrassment. For Jackson's inauguration, over 10,000 job seekers and revelers came to Washington, D.C., emptying the saloons of drink in a matter of days. After Jackson's inaugural speech, a huge crowd swarmed into the White House. They jumped on chairs, tore curtains, and smashed china. Jackson snuck out the back, not wishing to be with them. The only way the White House staff could get everyone to leave was to drag the hard liquor out to the front lawn. The revelers followed the alcohol, and the staff then locked the doors.

A People's Man and the Spoils System

In one real sense, Jackson was a "people's man." The term "Jacksonian Democracy" refers to expanding voting rights. During the Age of Jackson, voting eligibility expanded in all states so that all adult white men gained the right to vote. Property requirements for voting were abolished. Electors were democratically elected. Amidst this great expansion of the right to vote, women and non-whites still could not vote and 1/3 of the South were slaves with no rights. Still, nowhere else in the world offered this much democracy. Americans got the man and the party they chose.

Though it had existed before, Andrew Jackson perfected the "spoils system." To the victor goes the spoils. This means that the winner gets to reward those who supported him, and that supporters expect to get something in return for campaigning for someone. Jackson rewarded his supporters, and saw that this method of governing helped him maintain power. This meant, however, that government workers were not always the best suited or most capable for their jobs. And, the more people a president could hire, the more supporters he could count on in the following elections. Thus Jackson hired many people and his administration started the growth of the American government.

Jackson's "Kitchen Cabinet" were his closest advisors. Though known as a common man, Jackson chose the nation's elite to run his administration, including a newspaper editor, representatives of longstanding wealthy families, and his friends. His cabinet was somewhat dysfunctional because of a scandal involving the wife of his Secretary of War John Eaton. Peggy Eaton's first husband reportedly committed suicide because of his wife's affairs. Mrs. Eaton had such a bad reputation that other cabinet wives would not talk to her. Vice President John C. Calhoun's wife refused to travel to Washington, D.C. so she would not have to meet Mrs. Eaton.

Indian Fighter and Constitution Basher

Much of the story of relations between the United States of America and the various Indian tribes is based on the actions of Andrew Jackson and the fledgling Democratic Party. Jackson and the Democrats were intent on moving all Indians west of the Mississippi River, regardless of state law, federal law, Congress, and the Constitution. Because of Jackson's ruthless will, he was successful.

Though there were many Indian tribes affected by Jackson's policy, the Cherokee Indians give us an example of the raw political and military power that President Jackson used and abused. Americans called the Cherokee the "civilized tribe" because they had adopted Christianity and Western ways, had their own alphabet, their own constitution, farms, wooden houses, etc. However, the Cherokee had fought with the British in the American Revolution, and many Americans sought vengeance.

Along with Jackson, state leaders of Georgia, Mississippi, and Alabama all wanted the Indians out. However, legally, under the Constitution and federal treaties, the Indians had the right to stay. In addition, the President of the United States of America is not allowed to use federal force within a state without a law or emergency, so Jackson could not legally act. Then, in 1830, Congress passed the Indian Removal Act, which gave the president authority to remove Indians only when the Indians chose to relocate. Some Indians chose to leave, accepting $68 million from Georgia; however, thousands of Indians stayed.

In 1832, in Worcester v. Georgia, the Cherokee tribe challenged Georgia's violation of Indian land rights. Chief Justice Marshall and the Supreme Court ruled that Cherokee land rights were protected under the jurisdiction of the federal government. Jackson responded, "John Marshall has made his decision, now let him enforce it." Because the Supreme Court has no military and relies on the president to enforce the law, and because Jackson wanted his will carried out, one of the greatest tragedies caused by the American government occurred.

President Jackson and later President Van Buren ordered the U.S. Army to forcefully relocate Indians west of the Mississippi River on what historians call "The Trail of Tears." Approximately 20,000 Indians (including the Cherokee, Muscogee, Seminole, Chickasaw, and Choctaw nations) had chosen not to leave their native lands. American soldiers force-marched these Indians over 2,000 miles in some instances. The old and the very young were the first to die. President Van Buren ordered General Winfield Scott to remove 12,000 Cherokee. Over 3,000 died on the way. At each stop, Indians buried 15-20 Indians.

Jackson and Van Buren broke state law, federal law, and the Constitution, in ordering the U.S. Army to relocate Indians. They violated state law because the president is not allowed to order military action within a state without an act of Congress. Each state has authority over its own territory. They acted against federal law, because the Indian Removal Act allowed the president to remove Indians only if the Indians chose to relocate. They acted against the Constitution because the Indians had proven their case to the Supreme Court in Worcester v. Georgia. Jackson's action against the Indians was a presidential power grab against the Constitution and against the states.

INTERNAL IMPROVEMENTS

Under President Jackson, the federal government spent more money ($10 million) than all other administrations combined on internal improvements, such as roads and harbors. James Monroe had specifically denied projects which were not related to national defense, because defense projects are the only ones authorized by the Constitution. However, Jackson saw these building projects as ways to reward his political supporters. He did veto the Maysville Road Bill of 1830, but that was only because it was in Kentucky and would have benefitted his political rival, Henry Clay.

THE NULLIFICATION CRISIS

President Jackson was completely in support of an indivisible United States of America. As a boy, he acted courageously against the British in the American Revolution. He fought for many years against the Indians. In the War of 1812, he led the Americans to destroy the British at the Battle of New Orleans. There are many incidents where Jackson showed his loyalty toward his soldiers, acting bravely and sacrificing for others. Jackson was willing to put his life in danger for his country.

As president, Jackson supported an indivisible United States of America, even showing he was willing to invade a state and kill Americans to defend it. During his presidency, the country almost split in two, and a civil war nearly resulted. The Tariff of 1828 increased taxes on imported manufactured goods, which economically benefitted the North and hurt the South. Vice President John C. Calhoun and Southerners hated the tariff, but Jackson sided with federal law this time. At a dinner, Jackson raised his glass and gave a toast, "Our Union. It must be preserved." Calhoun retorted, "The Union, next to our liberty most dear!"

Southerners correctly saw the Tariff of 1828 as a challenge to their idea of states' rights. Southerners wanted to protect slavery, and realized that eventually the free states would outnumber the Southern states, and that Northerners would eventually make slavery illegal everywhere. A civil war nearly occurred at that time. South Carolina held a state convention in 1832 and nullified the tariff (declared the law did not exist within South Carolina). Calhoun resigned as vice president to support South Carolina. Then, Congress passed the Force Act of 1833 granting Jackson authority to use force to make South Carolina collect the tariff taxes. Jackson declared, "Nullification is incompatible with the existence of the Union. Disunion by armed force is treason." The crisis was averted only by a compromise tariff bill championed by Calhoun, Daniel Webster, and Henry Clay. The issue of slavery was again pushed out of the way.

Jackson's War on the Bank of the U.S.

Andrew Jackson opposed the Bank of the U.S. largely because he could not control it. The bank was run by Nicolas Biddle, who was appointed by James Monroe in 1823. Biddle did not owe allegiance to Jackson and hired whomever he wanted. The U.S. Bank was the third largest employer of the federal government, behind the military and the Post Office. Jackson wanted the Democrats to control who worked in the bank.

Jackson tried to kill the U.S. Bank and replace it with a banking system he controlled. In 1832, Congress passed reauthorization of the U.S. Bank, but Jackson vetoed it. (Jackson vetoed more bills than all other previous presidents combined.) Jackson claimed he did not trust bankers and supported the "Common Man," but in reality he wanted to control the bank. Jackson then removed all federal deposits from the bank and placed the money in smaller state banks controlled by Jackson's supporters. Two of Jackson's Secretaries of the Treasury refused to remove the deposits because they believed this action was unconstitutional, but Jackson fired both of them. Jackson soon named a man who also advocated removing the deposits, Roger Taney, as Chief Justice of the Supreme Court. The press called the new banks "pet banks." In 1836, authorization of the Bank of the U.S. ended, and with it, the Bank of the U.S. In 1837, an economic depression ensued, but historians argue over the main cause of this crisis.

Jackson and Big Government

Jackson expanded the power of the president and the federal government more than any other president before him. He used the spoils system to create a large-scale bureaucracy that weakened states' rights. For political parties to compete against the Democrats, they had to become more like the Democrats. The birth of the modern Democratic Party under Martin Van Buren fostered a corrupt new two-party system and bolstered slavery. Martin Van Buren forbade Democrats to take a strong stand against or for slavery, so that both Southerners and Northerners would vote for Democrats. This meant that politicians tried to ignore the issue of slavery, though slavery eventually would become too big a problem to ignore. Under Jackson, the federal government grew at an amazing rate. U.S. federal expenditures rose from $26 million in 1829 to $50 million in 1837. During Jackson's presidency, the government doubled in size relative to the population growth. From 1809 to 1841, the government grew five times in size.

UNIT VIII

EMPIRE OF LIBERTY OR MANIFEST DESTINY, 1836-1848

INTRODUCTION

To understand much of American history throughout the 1800s, it is important to grasp the meaning of two terms: Empire of Liberty and Manifest Destiny. Close in meaning, these ideas spurred immigrants from every continent of the world to move west and settle the western frontier. These two concepts encouraged Americans to believe it was their right to move west, remove Indians off of their land, defeat Mexico in a war, and establish the modern world's strongest republic.

Thomas Jefferson imagined the United States of America as an ever-expanding Empire of Liberty. This republic of farmer-citizens would offer the world a respite from the despotic governments that mark the history of mankind. Jefferson envisioned an America free from slavery, where people of all races and ethnicities would peacefully live with the liberties described in the Declaration of Independence and the Constitution. For many Americans, this vision of America was their guiding light throughout the 1800s. Even today, this vision is an entirely positive concept and inspires Americans.

Manifest Destiny is based on an older idea, beginning when the first Europeans colonized North and South America. From the 15th through the 17th centuries, Europeans led by Spain, Portugal, Great Britain, and France believed it was their God-given destiny to spread their culture throughout the world. Each believed that God gave them the right to bring their language, religion, and customs to the colonized lands. Spain, Portugal and France brought Catholicism; Great Britain brought Protestant Christianity. Each country brought its own language and customs.

In the 1800s, an American journalist coined the phrase "Manifest Destiny" during the Mexican-American War. Journalists, writers, and politicians believed that the United States of America was destined to rule America, from the Atlantic Ocean to the Pacific Ocean. Westward expansion had problems. The Democratic Party favored the expansion of slavery; the Whig Party opposed slavery. Manifest Destiny includes ideas that are negative, such as the subjugation of Native Americans, and in the South, the continuation of slavery.

A new kind of American, the westerner, emerged in 1800s America. Confident of his rights won by the American Founding Fathers, hopeful for the future, eager to enjoy the benefits of a plentiful country, and emboldened by a Christian faith that encouraged hard work, the westerner valued merit over family name and achievement over class. This American of the first half of the 1800s expanded America's borders to the Pacific Ocean. However, neither the westerners nor the Americans east of the Appalachian Mountains resolved the crisis of slavery.

CHAPTER 44

Change in America: Industrialization, Religion, and Social Change

From 1800 to 1850, life drastically changed for many Americans. In 1800, approximately 90% of Americans worked in farming. By 1850, only 64% worked in farming. The move from farms to cities created many problems; however, the standard of living greatly increased for the majority of Americans. Instead of laboring on a farm for one's food, Americans had time for other pursuits, like leisure, creating art, writing novels and pursuing a deeper understanding of God.

Along with the Industrial Revolution, there were other factors that brought change to life in America. One was a religious movement called the Second Great Awakening. Another was that for the first time since the Roman Republic, a nation existed on Earth whose people had the liberty to decide how their government would work and who would lead it. Moreover, Americans enjoyed the greatest economic freedoms in the world. Americans, spurred by these factors, created one of the most rapid increases in the standard of living of a people in history. At the same time as Americans were creating the freest and one of the most advanced societies on Earth, they also enslaved millions of people. The paradox of slavery existing in the world's freest country would remain America's greatest problem of the 1800s.

Many historians call this era the Age of Jackson, or Jacksonian Democracy. And while it is true that Andrew Jackson was a reason for the change, and while he does in many ways capture the mood of the times, he was not the main cause of the movements sweeping across America.

During the first half of the 1800s, Americans settled in greater numbers in cities. The growth of cities had a major effect on every aspect of American life. Below is a small list of cities and their growth from 1800 to 1850:

	1800	**1850**
NEW YORK	60,515	515,547
PHILADELPHIA	41,220	121,376
BOSTON	24,937	136,881
BALTIMORE	26,514	169,054
CINCINNATI	not founded in 1800	115,435
ST. LOUIS	not founded in 1800	77,860

Although industrialization created problems, it increased the standard of living for the average person. For the first time in America, large numbers of people had time for pursuits other than working to provide food and shelter.

THE SECOND GREAT AWAKENING, 1800-1850

America's Second Great Awakening was the birth of a particularly American democratic version of Christianity, and it included an explosion of various Protestant sects. Christian ministers broke traditions, founded sects, and appealed to the masses of common folk through various methods, including highly charged emotional preaching and singing. Charles Wesley of the Methodists (a religion formed in the early 1700s) adapted English pub songs for church! By 1844, the Methodist Church was the largest in the country.

The Second Great Awakening featured powerful speakers, outdoor events that would last for days, and emotionally-charged talks to sway people towards Jesus Christ. At these events, some attendees were inspired to move, fall, jerk, laugh, or cry during services. Participants were encouraged to pledge their lives to Jesus, to declare that Jesus Christ is the son of God, and thus to be saved from the fires of hell.

New religions sprang up, including varieties of Baptists, Presbyterians, and Congregationalists, and including a religion that claims that Jesus visited North America two thousand years ago (The Church of Jesus Christ of Latter-Day Saints, also known as the Mormons). One can see the results of this today, where one small town may have a dozen or more Christian denominations and churches, each promoting a slightly different brand of Christianity.

Because of the great diversity of Protestant Christian religions, Americans became extremely sensitive to religious tolerance towards other Christian faiths, except toward Catholics. Catholic Christians were seen as outsiders, a religious sect led by ancient Roman traditions and ceremonies. However, the Catholics were highly successful in converting American Indians to Christianity.

Utopian Socialist Movements

The 1800s was a time where a great number of idealists attempted to form perfect societies, or utopias. In nearly all of these societies, members founded communities based on socialist or communist ideals. These groups rejected the traditional Christian understanding of man, private property, and traditional family relationships. Many believed that humans did not need families, rules, private property, authority, and structure. Some believed that God or religion was unnecessary. Most if not all of the nonreligious communes failed for lack of food. Some communes were religious, including communes of the Shakers, the Amish, and the Mennonites. The Mormons adapted some forms of communalism. Some of these religious communes succeeded.

Socialist Robert Owen believed it was possible to educate individualism out of people. In founding the "New Harmony" settlement in Indiana, he promised to destroy the "Three-Headed Hydra: God, marriage, property." He imagined adults never marrying, but having countless partners, and the entire community raising children together. Owen invested what would amount to hundreds of millions in today's dollars. New Harmony ran out of food, and the people left.

Others founded communities based on similar ideas and met a similar fate—failure. John Noyes founded a community which rejected the notion of private property and promoted polygamous marriages. Transcendentalists founded two societies (Fruitland and Brook Farm) based on radical individualism, nonconformity, meditation, God in nature, and perpetual inspiration. The Shakers founded a community based on property sharing, vegetarianism, and abstinence from sex. This last community had problems sustaining a population.

Successful communes included the religious communities of the Amish and the Mennonites, founded on the principles of Christianity. The Amish are Protestant Christians who established communities in Pennsylvania beginning in the early 1700s. The Amish live simply, do not use many modern conveniences (such as cars), and have plain dress. The Amish continue to work closely with their neighbors in many areas of life and base their community on the teachings of Christ in the New Testament. The Mennonites are another Christian community, also established in the 1700s in Pennsylvania. Both the Amish and the Mennonites are pacifists and will not participate as soldiers in wars.

WOMEN'S RIGHTS

Throughout the 1800s, American women gained rights in nearly all areas of life. The United States of America became the world leader in the amount and kinds of rights women had. Although at the founding of the United States women did not have equal rights with men, the principles the country were founded on eventually extended to all people. In parts of the country, women gained property rights, and access to schools and professions. Women became key leaders in the temperance movement, which aimed to make alcohol illegal. In 1851, Maine prohibited alcohol in large part because of women's campaigns.

Feminism in America originated in the first half of the 1800s. Sarah and Angeline Grimke, Lucy Stone, Elizabeth Cady Stanton, Lucretia Mott and others gathered in Seneca Falls, New York in 1848 and issued the "Declaration of Sentiments," a document that declared women should have equal rights with men. Key feminist issues can be found in this important document, including women's lack of education, economic opportunities, legal rights, marital power, and the right to vote. This also set the agenda for future feminists.

The one feminist issue today that was not part of the Seneca Falls Convention is abortion. Feminist leaders in the 1800s saw abortion as murder. Elizabeth Cady Stanton, a mother of seven, wrote, "There must be a remedy for such a crying evil as this." Victoria Woodhull wrote, "Wives deliberately permit themselves to become pregnant of children and then, to prevent becoming mothers, as deliberately murder them while yet in their wombs." Dr. Elizabeth Blackwell, the country's first woman to earn a medical degree, wrote, "The gross perversion and destruction of motherhood by the abortionist filled me with indignation."

Abolitionism

Abolitionism was the movement to immediately end slavery everywhere in America. It is different from the political movement to keep slavery from expanding. Abolitionism existed in the United States of America from the beginning of the country. At the Continental Congress, Thomas Jefferson and other Founding Fathers attempted to get rid of slavery in the territories. Jefferson's first draft of the Declaration of Independence included statements that condemned slavery. One of the first laws of the new U.S. Congress was the Northwest Ordinance of 1787, which outlawed slavery north of the Ohio River. Abolitionists created societies to work together to end slavery, such as the Society for the Relief of Free Negroes Unlawfully Held in Bondage, established in Philadelphia in 1775.

Leaders in the Abolitionist movement included runaway slaves, former slaveholders, Northerners and Southerners. William Lloyd Garrison published an abolitionist newspaper, The Liberator. The Grimke sisters were daughters of a former slave owner. Once their father died, they freed all their slaves, moved to the North, and toured, giving speeches to persuade others to oppose slavery. Frederick Douglass, Sojourner Truth, and Harriet Tubman were escaped slaves who spoke and wrote about the horrors of slavery.

Abolitionists in the South and North participated in a transportation system called the Underground Railroad that secretly moved slaves into the free North and later into Canada. The Underground Railroad did not have real tracks and time schedules. Instead, it was a system of families who provided food, shelter, prayer, and encouragement to escaped slaves. Escaped slaves would travel by night. By day, escapees hid in abolitionist homes, called "Stations." Usually, an escaped slave was led by someone, called a conductor, who had made the journey before.

It is believed that from 1800 to 1865, over 100,000 slaves escaped along the Underground Railroad. The most well-known conductor was Harriet Tubman (1822?-1913). Tubman was beaten as a young slave, and suffered a traumatic head injury. As a young married woman, she escaped, though her husband, also a slave, chose not to leave. If caught, escaped slaves were tortured and sometimes killed. Once free, Tubman returned to the South over a dozen times to help her parents and approximately 70 other slaves get to freedom. Throughout the South, Tubman was wanted, dead or alive.

THE AMERICAN RENAISSANCE: ARTS AND LITERATURE

Before the 1800s, North America did not have its own distinct literary and artistic culture outside of political and religious documents. From the establishment of the first English settlement in America (Jamestown in 1607) through the end of the American Revolution (1783), nearly all inhabitants of America were engaged in a struggle for life and death or in a struggle for independence. The first colonies faced unbelievable challenges from nature, from Indians, in establishing a working colonial structure, and in breaking away from Great Britain. Disease and nature were perhaps the greatest obstacles to survival. Because of these difficulties, Americans did not have the time and leisure required to develop a high level of arts and literature. Americans needed to clear the fields and work the farms and could not spend their time on books and art.

A distinct American literature did develop throughout the first half of the 1800s. Authors wrote stories where nature, God, morality, love, sin, and individualism played key roles. American authors wrote stories that continue to appeal to the masses even today. Washington Irving (1783-1859) set his most well-known stories *Rip van Winkle* and *The Legend of Sleepy Hollow* in the countryside of upstate New York. He was America's first international best-selling author. James Fenimore Cooper (1789-1851) created the western-genre novels. His novel *The Last of the Mohicans* (1826) focused on frontiersmen, Indians, wily Frenchmen, dangers of the wild, and damsels in distress. Herman Melville (1819-1891) wrote *Moby Dick* and *Billy Budd*. His stories are a testament to the toughness of the 1800s American and deal with moral challenges of men, especially while at sea. *The Scarlet Letter* by Nathaniel Hawthorne (1804-1864) is a story of love, guilt, forgiveness, and redemption. Edgar Allan Poe (1809-1849) created the horror short story, the detective short story, and is most well-known for his poems and stories of mystery and the macabre.

Poets of the 1800s include Henry Wadsworth Longfellow (1807-1882) and Ralph Waldo Emerson (1803-1882). Longfellow lives on in *The Midnight Ride of Paul Revere*, which immortalized Mr. Revere and the fight of the average American against the mighty British Empire. Even though Emerson was a poet, he was primarily known for his ideas regarding individualism, nature, and his work as a leader of the Transcendentalists.

American painters of the 1800s created art that focused on the immense natural beauty of America and was enjoyed by the masses in both the U.S.A. and in Europe. The amazing vistas of the American West, the exotic nature of the Indians, and the wild and novel animals captured the imagination of both artists and average citizens. Painters such as George Caleb Bingham, Thomas Cole, and George Innes painted scenes of landscape art. These artists, and members of the Hudson River School, captured the breathtaking and inspiring natural beauty of America.

Chapter 45

Education in Early America through the Civil War

Education in America was, for the most part, accessible and affordable from the 1600s through most of the 1800s. Simple reading, writing, and arithmetic were essential to live in America. In the 1800s, hundreds of colleges opened throughout the country. Because the English colonists in the 1600s and 1700s were primarily Protestant Christians, they believed strongly in the individual's need to read the Bible, and to tie education with teaching moral principles founded on Christianity. It was the duty and religious desire of all good parents to teach their children how to read. Also, over 90% of British colonists in North America were small farmers who owned and worked on their own land. To survive, they needed to understand and use arithmetic. Most teaching and learning occurred in the home, and relative to the world, the typical American of the mid-1800s was well-educated.

Americans had great freedom in the methods and content of their education. As during the colonial period, American education for boys in towns and cities often consisted of becoming an apprentice to a master tradesman. Boys often lived in the master's home and worked under his guidance for seven years. At the end of the term, the apprentice would then become a master in that field of work, such as a silversmith, blacksmith, carpenter, or printer.

American girls of the 1800s learned basic reading, writing, and arithmetic, but also learned the homemaking skills of managing a household, sewing, cooking, and planning the lives of all the children. Before the 1830s, girls were not allowed in public schools. Mothers were in charge of religious education for the household. The typical American woman was expected to not only understand the basics of her husband's or future husband's work, but was also trained to keep the family clothed, fed, clean, and on task. In today's understanding, it may sound as if the 1800s woman's life was limited, but before the Industrial Revolution, both male and female roles were limited because life was one of constant struggle against nature and scarcity, and the work of both husband and wife was necessary to survive.

Americans of the 18th and 19th century had a working knowledge of the English language, with literacy rates among whites at 97% in the mid-1800s. However, Americans read widely, but not deeply. Most Americans read politics and economics from newspapers. They read almanacs to improve farming. Americans did not read novels as Europeans did and thus lacked a deep knowledge of philosophy and literature. Slaves were not allowed to read and write, and were kept uneducated by their masters as a way to control them.

During the debate regarding the acceptance or denial of the Constitution, Alexander Hamilton, John Jay, and James Madison wrote a series of essays entitled *The Federalist Papers* aimed at the American urban professional. These essays are complex, by our standards, and are taught at the university level.

Common books in elementary schools and in the home were Noah Webster's *Blue-Backed Speller* and *McGuffey's Readers*. Initially, Webster's books focused on religious themes. Webster attempted to promote republican virtues and values to strengthen the American system of government. *McGuffey's Readers*, written for grades 1-6, were perhaps the most used schoolbooks of the 1800s. *McGuffey's Readers* taught all subjects with the intention of promoting Protestant Christian beliefs and manners in all students. In the 1836-1837 edition, Christian themes of salvation, righteousness, and piety were prominent.

The male elite in America had what is called a Classical Education. Though taught in the home from an early age, by the age of 11 or 12, these individuals had private tutors, and learned classical languages, such as Greek and Latin, and mastery of English grammar. Well-educated Americans were expected to read classical literature, and many were able to read in the language of the novelist. By age 15, a few American young men were sent to Europe to learn in European colleges. Both in Europe and America, study was focused on reading and discussing great literature, learning languages, and searching for the truth. Religion and faith were instrumental in education as morality was taught as a part of academics.

COLLEGES

Americans established a tremendous number of colleges in the 1800s. By 1861, more than 600 colleges had been founded since the beginning of the republic. Today, 182 of these colleges still survive. Nearly all of the American colleges of the 18th and 19th centuries were religious. In contrast to the colleges in Europe, colonial colleges were private (not funded and controlled by the state or government) and therefore, independent and reliant on donations. Americans continued this trend in establishing colleges throughout the 1800s.

In addition to private colleges, Americans formed state colleges. The Northwest Ordinance of 1787 established the Northwest Territory and stated, "Religion, morality, and knowledge, being necessary to good government and the happiness of mankind, schools and the means of education shall forever be encouraged." American Founding Fathers believed that religion and morality were essential parts of a thriving republic, because in a free republic, virtue is required to guide the morality of the citizens. The founders also believed that public education should be supported by federal law. The first state school in the Northwest was Ohio University. Other state schools followed. State schools focused on teaching agriculture and technical professions.

Various Christian religions founded most of America's colleges with the aim of serving all with the Christian faith as a guide. Christian colleges led the way in admitting women and blacks, and in providing intellectual power to reform movements such as freeing the slaves and striving for equal rights for women. The first college to admit women and African-Americans was Oberlin College, founded by Presbyterians in 1833 in Ohio.

Early colleges in America were founded primarily to teach ministers, but they offered a broad education also suitable for teachers, lawyers, and businessmen. The first colleges in America were:

COLLEGE	YEAR	FOUNDERS
Harvard College	1636	Puritan (Congregationalist)
College of William and Mary	1693	Church of England
Yale College	1701	Puritan (Congregationalist)
Princeton University	1746	Presbyterian
Columbia College	1754	Church of England
University of Pennsylvania	1755	Church of England
Brown University	1764	Baptist
Queen's College	1766	Dutch Reformed
Dartmouth College	1769	Puritan (Congregationalist)

HORACE MANN AND PUBLIC SCHOOLS

While serving in a variety of political and educational roles in Massachusetts, Horace Mann (1796-1859) was a leading spokesman for a publicly-funded school system. As the Secretary of the Massachusetts State Board of Education, Mann wanted an educational system that included health and physical education, academic education, and music education, but most importantly, Mann wanted American education to inculcate moral, ethical, and political values that promote democracy. He believed that Americans educated in academics and moral principles would make for a stronger republic. Mann wanted the education to be for both boys and girls.

Some of Horace Mann's educational philosophy was influenced by his travels abroad. In 1843, Mann traveled to Prussia, a military state tightly run by King Frederick William IV. The Prussian school system was designed to train Prussians to be loyal, obedient, and efficient citizens and bureaucrats of the state. The state supported the schools, trained and paid the teachers, and all students were mandated to attend up to a certain age. Schools were secular, though patriotism to the state was taught as a core principle. Mann agreed with many aspects of the Prussian school system, but thought the Prussian system did not support representative democracy.

In 1852, Mann supported the decision in Massachusetts to adopt a publicly-funded, mandatory public education system. Soon after, New York adopted a similar system. Over time, each state passed laws that made education publicly-funded and mandatory. For the most part, Americans agreed to this idea, even though some parents resisted because they did not want to give up moral education to unknown teachers and bureaucrats. For his work, Horace Mann is called "the father of American public education."

CHAPTER 46

THE SOUTHWEST AND THE WAR FOR TEXAS INDEPENDENCE (1835-1836)

Until the Mexican-American War ended in 1848, the Southwest and California were sparsely-inhabited lands. Thousands of Native Americans had lived in this area before the arrival of the Spanish. The American Indians lived as farmers, hunters, and gatherers.

From the 1500s on, Spanish explorers and Catholic missionaries explored and established religious missions. The Spanish intermarried with the Indians and established ranches. Catholic Jesuit priests converted the Indians to Catholic Christianity, and over time, the Spanish culture replaced the Indian culture. The most well-known of these missionaries was Father Junipero Serra (1713-1784), who began the California mission system consisting of 21 missions along the coast, each a one-day walking distance from the next.

In 1821, Mexico gained its independence from Spain, and took control of all of California and the Southwest. Mexico secularized all religious properties. This meant that the Mexican state took all church property. From 1821 on, the Mexican government attempted to encourage settlement of its northern lands, but Mexicans did not resettle. By the time of the Mexican-American War, there were approximately 10,000 inhabitants of California and the Southwest, not including those in Texas.

WAR FOR TEXAS INDEPENDENCE (1835-1836)

The history of the War for Texas Independence starts with the birth of the country of Mexico in 1821. In that year, the Mexicans defeated Spain and established a republic. In many ways, Mexicans wanted to have a republic like the U.S.A. The new government encouraged Mexicans to move north, into the land of Texas and what is now the Southwest of the U.S.A. However,

Mexicans did not want to move. To occupy this land and build a prosperous nation, the Mexican government advertised for Americans to move to Texas.

Mexico made a deal with potential American settlers of Texas: Move to Mexico, live and work tax free, and you will be Mexican citizens, as long as you:
1. Become Catholic
2. Speak and write Spanish at all times in public
3. Not keep slaves

The Mexicans made Stephen Austin (1793-1836) the director of American immigration into Texas, and 20,000 Americans had moved to Texas by 1831. However, Mexico did not enforce its own laws, and the Americans remained Protestant Christians, spoke and wrote English at all times, and kept slaves. This angered the Mexican government and caused a reaction.

To stop American immigration into Mexico, Mexicans passed the Mexican Colonization Act of 1830. This Act forbade Americans from moving into Mexico and banned slavery. Despite the new law, Americans continued to flow into Mexico, only now they came as illegal aliens. With the passage of the Colonization Act, Texans started to organize an independence movement.

Mexico had changed governments many times and the political situation was unstable. One of Mexico's top generals, Santa Anna (1794-1876), was power-hungry, and eventually destroyed the Mexican Republic and made himself dictator. Perhaps because of this, Texans thought they could assert themselves.

In 1835, Santa Anna decided to teach the Texans a lesson and reassert Mexican control by marching his army into Texas. One of the early battles was at the Alamo, February 23 to March 6, 1836. The Alamo was a small mission in the south of Texas. Approximately 187 Texans had positioned themselves at the Alamo, hoping to slow down Santa Anna's march north. Legendary figures of the American West were present, including Davey Crockett, Jim Bowie, and Colonel William B. Travis. Seeing their position as hopeless, Travis proclaimed, "Let's make their victory worse than defeat."

Santa Anna was corrupt and disliked by his own soldiers. His army was undisciplined, and it is believed that Santa Anna did not apply himself to the military task at hand, but wasted time during the siege of the Alamo. Santa Anna and his army of 4,000 took more than one week to defeat the 187 Texans. In the end, Mexicans killed all Texan combatants at the Alamo, but it is believed the Texans killed from 400 to 1,600 Mexicans, and they succeeded in slowing down Santa Anna's march north. When news reached the other Texans about the brave stance at the Alamo, "Remember the Alamo" became an inspiring rally cry for Texans to volunteer and defeat Santa Anna.

During the siege of the Alamo, Texans met at a convention and adopted the Texas Declaration of Independence on March 2, 1836. Sam Houston (1793-1863) was chosen to be in charge of an army. Houston guessed that his army of volunteers would last for only one battle, and he was cautious to not be caught off-guard by Santa Anna. At the same time, Santa Anna thought the Texans were near defeat. He split his army in two, and both Mexican armies searched southeast Texas for Houston's army.

Though Houston escaped capture and detection for over a month, Mexican forces won another battle at Goliad, in late March of 1836. Under the command of Colonel Jose Nicolas de la Portilla, soldiers brutally massacred the Texan prisoners of war. Portilla took between 425 and 445 Texans and marched them between two rows of Mexican soldiers ordered to shoot the prisoners point blank. Survivors were clubbed and knifed to death. The Mexicans piled the dead bodies and burned them, leaving the remains for animals.

On April 21, Houston's army of 900 men engaged Santa Anna's forces of

700 at the Battle of San Jacinto, and in 18 minutes, the Texans defeated the Mexicans, and the war was over. The next day, Texans caught Santa Anna, who had disguised himself as a peasant. Houston forced Santa Anna to sign a treaty which recognized Texas as an independent country, with the Rio Grande as the southern border. Returning to Mexico City, Santa Anna was disgraced and deposed, and Mexico repudiated the treaty. Houston and the Texans immediately applied to the United States Congress for admission as a state, but were rejected.

CHAPTER 47

PRESIDENCIES OF VAN BUREN (1837-1841), HARRISON (1841), AND TYLER (1841-1845)

Martin Van Buren, architect of the modern Democratic Party and the spoils system, was in many ways an unlikely president to follow in the footsteps of Andrew Jackson. Van Buren was from the greatest metropolis in America, New York City. Unlike Jackson, he was not a common man from the West. He was a career politician, holding office since the age of 18. Unlike Jackson, he had never fought in war or against Indians, owned no slaves, and personally hated the peculiar institution of slavery. However, Van Buren had created the political machine that won the election for Jackson, and his own presidency was seen as inevitable by the Democrats.

Van Buren's presidency was crippled by the Panic of 1837, an unprecedented economic depression. This depression, and Van Buren's inability to connect with Americans, made his a one-term presidency (the first one-term presidency since the Adams family). Americans suffered a 30% unemployment rate, cotton and wheat prices fell, banks foreclosed on homes and farms, and property values decreased. Van Buren believed that one solution to the problem was for America to hold deposits, and thus he created the U.S. Treasury.

Many historians believe Jackson's destruction of the Bank of the U.S. was the cause of Panic of 1837 depression, but most likely there were other reasons. For decades before the 1837 crash, Mexicans, flush with silver from Mexican mines, had come to Santa Fe to purchase American products. This fueled the American economy. After the War for Texas Independence (1835-1836), the Mexican government did not want to do business with America. Demand for American products fell, and manufacturers were stuck with products on their shelves. Even in the country's infancy, Americans lived in an interconnected world, whether they realized it or not.

HARRISON AND TYLER

William Henry Harrison owns the distinction of being the first American president to die in office. He delivered his inaugural address in a cold wind, caught pneumonia, and died within a month of becoming president. Succeeding him was Vice President John Tyler.

In the Age of Jackson, the opposition party to the Democrats was the Whig Party. The Whigs in America saw themselves as opposing the strong presidency that Jackson and the Democrats had created. Although the Whigs were against building up the power of the presidency as Jackson had done, they realized that they had to appeal to the masses in order to win. Harrison ran on his experience as an Indian fighter and hard-drinker. Harrison marketed his ticket as "Tippecanoe and Tyler, Too." "Old Tippecanoe" was a nickname he earned as the general who defeated the Shawnee Indians in 1811 at the Battle of Tippecanoe. When Van Buren's party tried to make Harrison appear as an alcoholic, Harrison's campaign bragged that he was not only an Indian fighter, but an able whiskey drinker. Tippecanoe's "Log Cabin Campaign" was a great success.

The lingering and negative effects of the Panic of 1837 dogged Tyler's presidency. The youngest to become president, at age 51, Tyler also made no friends during his tenure. Though Tyler's own party voted in Congress for a new Bank of the U.S., Tyler vetoed the bills sent to him and his entire cabinet resigned.

Throughout the turmoil of the economic depression, Americans pushed west and the country expanded and solidified its borders. Under Tyler, the Maine-Canada border was settled peacefully with Great Britain through the Webster-Ashburton Treaty (1842). Regardless of the president, Americans were rapidly settling the western territories and were interested in the Southwest and Northwest.

Chapter 48

Presidency of Polk (1845-1849) and the Mexican-American War (1846-1848)

In just one term, the 11th United States President, James K. Polk, succeeded in fulfilling his major campaign promises, nearly doubling the country's territory, and then he retired. Polk completed Jefferson's idea of the "Empire of Liberty" and the longer held notion of "Manifest Destiny" in a matter of a few years. However, the addition of new territory, both in the North and the South, and the end of western expansion, would bring the country's attention back to the issue that would eventually split the country in two. Polk's successes in territorial expansion exacerbated the contentious slavery issue. After Polk, the country would jump into war against itself in a mere 12 years.

The pro-slavery, southern Democrat Polk presidential campaign was based on completing the Manifest Destiny. Polk campaigned to annex Texas to the south and Oregon to the north, and made the election about expansion, not about slavery. Anti-slavery Whigs opposed annexation of Texas and slavery, but some pro-slavery Whigs wanted to annex the new land. The Whigs split in two, and Polk won the election. The Whigs lost because their candidate (Henry Clay) opposed annexing Texas but did not think of including Oregon as a free soil state. Polk's genius was combining both Texas as a slave state and Oregon as a free state in his campaign. Polk represented expansion.

A few days before Polk took office, the U.S. Congress wrote a bill to annex Texas. Southern politicians overwhelmingly wanted to admit the giant slave land, and Northerners greatly feared the ramifications of letting in a slave state nearly the size of Arkansas, Mississippi, Louisiana, and Alabama combined. However, in 1844, pro-slavery Secretary of State John C. Calhoun negotiated a treaty of annexation of Texas, with the Rio Grande River as the border, based on the treaty Texas had signed with Santa Anna. Mexico claimed the border was the Nueces River. In his last two months of office, President Tyler persuaded Congress to issue an annexation resolution. Months after Tyler left office and during Polk's presidency, Texas joined as a slave state on December 29, 1845.

With the annexation of Texas, war appeared inevitable with Mexico. After Polk was inaugurated president in March 1845, he sent Ambassador John Slidell to Mexico to offer a low price to buy the entire Southwest. Mexico broke off diplomatic relations with the U.S. Polk wanted to control all of the Southwest, and needed an excuse to act militarily. Mexico wanted to have Texas back, because they had never accepted the results of the War for Texas Independence. To "protect" Texas, Polk sent General Zachary Taylor, "Old Rough-and-Ready," to position troops in the disputed area, between the Nueces River and the Rio Grande River. Mexico sent its troops into the disputed area as well, and a fight broke out in July of 1845. Polk was ready for this incident, and had already sent an American fleet to California. Congress then declared war. Illinois Representative Abraham Lincoln and free state Whigs opposed the war, and southern Democrats supported the war.

Most in Europe believed that Mexico would win the war, with Mexican soldiers marching into the streets of Washington, D.C. Mexico's army was a permanent and large fixture in Mexican society, whereas the American army was all volunteers. However, there was much wrong with Mexico and its army. Frequent revolutions and changes in government made Mexico a weak country. The officer class consisted of wealthy Europeans and Mexicans, and leadership was not based on merit. Soldiers came from the poorest of the society, and were ill-equipped and poorly trained. Though numbering over 30,000, the Mexican Army lost every major battle against the smaller American forces. The Americans were all volunteers led by able officers trained at West Point Military Academy, where standards were rigorous. Thus, the Americans had a willing fighting force from a free republic and the Mexicans fielded a poorly-led, low-morale force of conscripts (draftees).

The United States of America was successful on land and sea, in Mexico and the Southwest. America hoped to end the war quickly, and schemed with exiled dictator Santa Anna, whom Mexico had forced to live in Cuba. America smuggled him back into Mexico with the stipulation that he would take charge and end the war. However, once in Mexico, Santa Anna declared he would fight "until death, to the defense of the liberty and independence of the republic."

During the war, Mexicans started calling the Americans "gringos" because the American soldiers liked to sing a song called "Green Grow the Lilacs." This pejorative term for Americans lives on in modern times.

Americans tried to force Mexico to surrender early, but the Mexican government would not give up. In 1847, American forces invaded and occupied Mexico City for many months, and conquered California and the Southwest. Marines guarded the National Palace, the "Halls of Montezuma" (as stated in the Marine Song), against vandals and thieves. Santa Anna, disgraced in battle again, escaped Mexico. The two most successful American generals in the war were Zachary Taylor, "Old Rough-and-Ready," and Winfield Scott, "Old Fuss and Feathers." Both Taylor and Scott were Whigs.

The terms of the treaty could be summed up as "spoils to the victors, but at a cost." The 1848 Treaty of Guadalupe Hidalgo gave all of the Southwest (today's Arizona, New Mexico, Utah and Nevada), California, and the disputed area in Texas to the United States of America. In return, America paid $15 million plus other payments. Part of the "other payments" were Mexican debts to Americans. During the war, the Mexican government had taken property in Mexico that was owned by Americans. The U.S.A. agreed to pay the Americans what Mexico owed them, which was an additional $3.2 million. (In today's money, $18 million would be equal to over $500 million.) This is a great deal of money, considering that Americans were the victors. The war cost nearly 13,000 American lives through battle and disease.

Was America justified in taking all of the Southwest and California (called the Mexican Cession) from Mexico? On one hand, Mexico held this territory only from 1821 to 1848. Before 1821, Spain controlled the area, and Mexico fought a war to take it from Spain, who had taken it from the Indians. If Mexico had the right to fight a war and take it from Spain, then by this same logic, the U.S.A. had the same right to fight Mexico and take the land. In addition, it is believed that only 10,000 Mexicans lived in the Mexican Cession. However, Mexico did not want to give the Americans this land, and ever since, Mexico has felt cheated by its neighbor to the north. Even today, one can hear the argument that California and the Southwest are really part of Mexico.

CHAPTER 49

THE CALIFORNIA GOLD RUSH AND THE OREGON TRAIL

The California Gold Rush was the key moment in immigration to California. In 1848, foreman John Marshall of Sutter's Mill saw something on the ground, most likely in a stream. It was a rock that sparkled in the sun. When he bent down, picked it up, and showed others, he not only was the proud owner of a piece of gold, but he had started a mad rush of hundreds of thousands to California. The gold had been found at Sutter's Mill, outside of Sacramento. Never again would California be a sleepy coastal territory.

The next year, in 1849, over 100,000 men rushed into California, hoping to strike it rich. These newcomers were called "49'ers," and very few of them found enough gold to make a living. There were three ways to get to California. The hardest way that a few attempted was going across the entire country on foot or horseback. The second route was by ship from major cities of the East Coast of the U.S. to the Panama Isthmus, then hiking across Panama, and taking a ship the rest of the way to California. This route included the danger of getting diseases in Panama. The third route was by ship from the East Coast around Cape Horn at the southern tip of South America, then north to California. The water at Cape Horn is extremely cold and stormy, and there was always a danger of dying at sea.

The men who went to California for gold stayed for the rich agriculture. Over 99.9% of those seeking gold went broke. Some left their wives, children, and farms to seek riches in California. However, once the gold diggers realized they were not going to get wealthy, they found a better source of economic opportunity: California farming. In many regions, the land was fertile and the water and sun were plentiful. California soon became a leader in the country's agricultural industry.

THE OREGON TRAIL

After the Lewis and Clark Expedition, explorers and trappers moved west into the Oregon Country by way of the Oregon Trail from 1811 to 1840. The trail was an approximately 2,000-mile-long route, beginning in Independence, Missouri, on the Missouri River, and ending in Oregon City, Oregon. Fur trappers and traders laid the trail wide enough for only one person to walk or ride on horseback. By 1836, the trail was wide enough to fit one wagon. From 1839 to 1846, about 6,000 pioneer families traveled on the Oregon Trail. Oregon had rich soil and an ample water supply for farmers. During this time, Methodist missionaries Marcus and Narcissa Whitman and 1,000 migrants tried to establish a mission to convert the Indians in present-day Washington state. Though the mission had some success during its 10 years, a measles epidemic wiped out many natives in 1847, and the Indians then murdered the Whitmans. In the Rocky Mountains, Jesuit Catholic missionaries led by Father Pierre De Smet successfully established six missions.

The mass movement of people on the Oregon Trail started with the Oregon Treaty (1846). The Oregon Treaty established the 49th parallel as the boundary between Great Britain to the north and the U.S.A. to the south, in Oregon Territory. From 1846 to 1869, hundreds of thousands of Americans braved the dangers along the Oregon Trail in order to start farms and communities in the Northwest. Mormons traversed the Oregon Trail, then veered south on the Mormon Trail and established Utah. Many others continued on the California Trail. The effort and actions of these Americans moving west brought great change to North America in the 1800s. Starting in 1869, many Americans migrated west along the transcontinental railroad.

Travelers on the Oregon Trail experienced great sadness, exhaustion, and exhilaration. Families often journeyed together in what was called a wagon train. In larger groups, families could defend themselves from the hardships of nature and disease, and from hostile Indians. The young, old, weak, and unlucky frequently died on the trail. Anna Maria King wrote to her family in 1845 about her trip:

But listen to the deaths: Sally Chambers, John King and his wife, their little daughter Electa and their babe, a son 9 months old, and Dulancy C. Norton's sister are gone. Mr. A. Fuller lost his wife and daughter Tabitha. Eight of our two families have gone to their long home.

Despite the dangers, the typical Oregon Trail trek was simply a long and extremely difficult effort with potential for land and happiness at journey's end. Travelers were also amazed by the grandeur and beauty of the American West. Imagine gazing at the Rocky Mountains for the first time, or seeing lava beds from a volcanic eruption, or viewing the Columbia River Gorge. Reports of the incredible beauty, openness, and economic opportunity of the West inspired people from all over the world to come to America.

UNIT IX

SECTIONALISM

INTRODUCTION

Throughout the 1800s, the people of America could be described based on the section of the country in which they lived. In many ways, those of the North were distinct from those of the South, and people from the West were different than those from the other two sections of the country. Geography and climate are two reasons for these differences. However, the greatest reason the South differed from other areas of the country was due to the practice of slavery. Slavery affected every part of Southern life, and it affected how Southerners viewed and dealt with people from the rest of the country. As the young United States of America of 1800 changed over the next 60 years, it divided along the line between free and slave states until the country could not remain half free and half slave. The slave society of the South, and the moral and political problems it posed, became the main cause of our country's greatest war, the Civil War (1861-1865).

CHAPTER 50

THE SOUTH

GEOGRAPHY AND CLIMATE OF THE SOUTH

The South can be divided into various geographical regions: the Gulf Coast and Coastal Plains, the Piedmont, the Appalachian and Ozark Mountains, and the greater Mississippi River area. In the 1700s and 1800s, the geography and climate of each area determined the area's economy.

The Gulf Coast and Coastal Plains tend to be hot, humid, and flat, with the growing season extending to nine months. Because of the favorable farming conditions, plantations (giant Southern farms with many slaves) were located in the Gulf Coast and Coastal Plains regions, particularly in the Deep South. The Coastal Plains are flat for about 65 miles inland from the ocean. Winters are mild. This area is excellent for crops such as rice and cotton.

In most of the interior of the South, the conditions were not the best for plantations due to more rain, harsher winters, and in many places tornadoes that hit in November, March, and April. In these areas, white farmers made a living through subsistence farming, eating the crops they grew themselves. Piedmont means "foothills" in French, and the Piedmont lay in between the Atlantic Coastal Plain and the Appalachian Mountains. The Appalachian Mountains extend from Canada to north-central Alabama, and the Ozark Mountains are in Arkansas, Missouri, and Oklahoma. The Mississippi River was the transportation hub of the South, used as a link with the rest of the world as materials moved through New Orleans. The Mississippi Delta, an area from Memphis, Tennessee, to Natchez, Mississippi, was a rich cotton region.

THE SOUTHERN DEFENSE OF SLAVERY

In many ways, the Antebellum South (Pre-war South) resembled a medieval society. In medieval society, the nobility ruled the rest of the people, supported by religion and believing they alone could decide what was best for the poor, landless farmers known as serfs. It was nearly impossible to break into the upper classes. In the South, very large planters were about 1% of the population, but they controlled the land, the politics, and a great many people through their ownership of plantations (huge farms with over 50 slaves). Below the planters were smaller farmers, 16% of the population, who owned 1-5 slaves. Below this group were poor, white farmers, consisting of 50% of the Southern populace. And, at the bottom of this power pyramid were the black slaves, making up about 33% of the South's total population (about 13% of the entire U.S. population). For the most part, folks were born into their class and they died in it. The South relied on a strong government that kept 33% of its population in bondage and kept the ruling class in charge.

The rigid social and political structure of the South went against the founding principles of America and against capitalism. Thomas Jefferson wrote in the Declaration of Independence that "all men are created equal." Capitalism depends on the free choices made by individuals, acting on their own free will in a free market. It functions when the economic structure allows for all people to compete fairly. When 33% of society is not free, capitalism and liberty are severely limited.

The South's economy suffered from slavery. Although 1/3 of the people had absolutely no legal rights, the other 2/3 were also limited. Plantation profits averaged about 8.5%, whereas manufacturing profits were between 22% and 45%. The population of the South did not grow like the North's did. In 1860, the South had 9 million people, of these about 3.2 million were slaves, and the North had 22 million. Industry in the South was much less developed than in the North. The institution of slavery encouraged great evils among the white slave owners. Also, Southerners distorted Christianity in order to defend slavery. In true Christianity, every person is viewed as an equal, there are no privileged classes, and Christians are taught to be loving and forgiving of everyone.

Southerners who defended slavery did so on the grounds of supposed economic and social justice, religion, and a "live and let live" philosophy. Southern politician John C. Calhoun said, "Many…once believed that (slavery) was a moral and political evil; that folly and delusion are gone; we now see it in its true light…as the most safe and stable basis for free institutions in the world." Southerner George Fitzhugh wrote in his book *Cannibals All!* that nearly all blacks and whites should be slaves, because slaves were freed from decision making. He wrote, "Liberty is an evil which government is intended to correct." Fitzhugh envisioned an elite few making all decisions for society. His arguments were in line with many Socialist and Communist leaders today. Southern religious leaders rationalized slavery because they believed that through slavery, blacks learned about Christ. A common slaveholder had a different argument: "Who do they think they are to tell me what is right and wrong? Why don't they just mind their own business and not try to legislate morality?"

One major reason for the strong defense of slavery was the profit from cotton production. In 1793, Northern teacher Eli Whitney invented the cotton gin, a simple yet revolutionary machine that enabled one person to do the work of 50 in separating the seeds from cotton. Instantly, cotton became much more profitable. Cotton production as a percentage of United States' exports went from 7.1% in 1800 to 57.5% in 1860. One nickname of the South was the "Cotton Kingdom."

The institution of slavery required a strong government that controlled the lives of a large percentage of society. The goal of Southern law toward slaves was to control them through Slave Codes, or "Black Codes." Slaves were not allowed to learn to read and write, because reading and writing encourages thinking, dreaming, and organizing – and it allows for communication. If slaves wrote essays about why they should be free, it might change the minds and hearts of slave owners. Slaves were not allowed to own guns. With a gun, a slave would have been impossible to whip, beat, or to hurt in other ways. Toward the slave, Southern law was totalitarian. Pro-slavery Southerners argued that the slave had a better, safer life and needed laws. Slavery required a strong government to enforce its laws among freed people as well. Whites were compelled to serve in "Slave Patrols." Slave Patrols hunted runaway slaves and brought them back to their owners. In many cases, poor whites had to work for free, helping the rich plantation owners keep their "property."

Slaves had absolutely no rights, could be sold or traded at any time, and masters could do anything they wanted to their slaves. Many slave owners did not physically harm their slaves, either due to moral reasons or because slaves were expensive "property." However, some owners treated their slaves miserably, torturing and murdering them. About 1/3 of the time, a slave family was broken up, with the parents or children being sold to another slave owner. In most cases, no communication between slaves on different plantations was allowed. In addition, babies from a master-slave relationship were slaves, and female slaves were not allowed to refuse the advances of the master. Because of this, many slaves, including Frederick Douglass and Booker T. Washington, did not know who their white fathers were.

Life in the South

The majority of white people in the South (73%) did not own slaves. It was possible to grow up a Southerner and to have never even seen a slave. When the Civil War broke out, these Southerners fought bravely for their homeland, believing they were defending their state from the invading Northerners. To them, the war was not about slavery, but about fighting off an invading army. Most white Southerners had come from England and Scotland in the 1700s and early 1800s. Few later immigrants moved to the South, because they could not compete with slaves for work. Most immigrants lived in the North, where there was more opportunity for common white working folks.

Other white Southerners owned between 50 and 200 acres of land. These small farmers grew crops that they ate, and traded what was left over in local markets. Often, farmers bartered their crops with other merchants and workers for goods and services. One farmer might provide corn in return for renting a farm animal. These farmers were called subsistence farmers because they relied on their own crops, and on hunting and fishing, for the food they ate.

Life in the South was dominated by agriculture and livestock. There were few large cities. Even though there were large communities with no direct contact with slavery, slavery still impacted everyone's life. The South did not develop manufacturing and was not a destination for the immigrants to America. These facts kept the South isolated and backward. 84% of the country's large farms were located in the South. The South was responsible for 99.9% of the country's cotton production and had 71% of the donkeys and mules used for pulling plows. The South led the North in rice and tobacco production. Most of these products came from plantations, the large farms with 50 or more slaves. However, most of the people did not live on plantations.

Religion and family life were extremely important to Southerners. Southerners were primarily Protestant Christians, with Methodist, Baptist, and Presbyterian churches predominant. There were a small number of Catholics, and a smaller number of Jews. Slave owners taught their slaves about Christianity, but forbade their slaves to read and write. According to most Protestant Christians, a person needs to read the Bible on his own to be a good Christian, so the fact that slave owners taught their slaves about Christianity but forbade reading is a paradox.

Despite the slave masters' plan, religion was a radical force that gave slaves hope. Nearly all slaves converted from their various African polytheistic beliefs to Christianity. Many slaves prayed and hoped for freedom on Earth in their lifetime, and many thought it would come at the turn of the century (the year 1800). Slaves also used songs to express their hopes for freedom, singing about Moses freeing the Hebrews while thinking about God freeing the American slaves. These songs are known as spirituals, or gospel music.

CHAPTER 51

THE NORTH

GEOGRAPHY AND CLIMATE OF THE NORTH

The Northern states were composed of the Northeastern region, the Mid-Atlantic region, and what we today call the Midwest. The Northeast has warm, humid summers and cold, snowy winters. The short growing season and the cold make large-scale farming difficult. The Northeast also is hilly and rocky, with many fast-flowing streams. To the south, in the Mid-Atlantic, the winters are milder and the soil is fertile. The geography and climate of the Northeast was suited for the Industrial Revolution, which required rivers to power mills. The Northeastern climate also favored small dairy farms. The Midwest (which was the old Northwest) had ample forests, the Great Lakes, and thousands of smaller lakes and rivers.

The North's geographical features include low-lying mountains and rivers of all sizes. The Appalachian Mountains extend from Canada to Alabama. When snow melted in these mountains, it rushed down in streams and rivers. The flowing water was used to power mills. The Ohio, Mississippi, and Missouri Rivers were used as transportation highways. In addition, the Great Lakes and the Erie Canal brought goods to the business capital of the U.S., New York City.

LIFE IN THE NORTH

During the 1800s, Northerners experienced the fruits of liberty, small government, and capitalism. Slavery was outlawed in the North following the American Revolution. Because of this, there was less need for a large government to keep the slave structure intact. Immigrants from the world rushed into the North, creating a large population to fill the factory jobs. Investors searched for the highest profitable return on their investments, and the North saw great improvements in living standards because of the Industrial Revolution. Inventors and builders created some of the world's best farm and factory products.

The North's economy was much more diverse than the South's. Northerners were small farmers, factory workers, sailors, and ship builders. The majority of people were small farmers who owned their own land. However, in 1860, in the South over 90% were farmers, but in the North it was about 75%. The rest of the Northerners lived in urban areas and experienced the Industrial Revolution.

Because of the rocky and hilly areas of New England, many in these states had dairy farms. In the Midwest and the Mid-Atlantic states, the farmland was extremely fertile. Farmers grew fruits, vegetables, grains, poultry, and forest products. On the coast in New England, Americans built some of the world's finest ships, and American sailors were known as some of the best.

The Industrial Revolution brought historic change in how people worked and lived. It began in England and came to America. British inventors created machines that operated by manipulating the power of water, and these machines made it easier to make things. The first factories built in large numbers were textile mills, factories for making cloth. The factories provided a great attraction for many immigrants who came in the 1800s.

Americans also revolutionized transportation in the 1800s. Robert Fulton (1765-1815) improved the steam engine, which established a profitable and efficient means of transporting people using steam power. His steamboat called The North River Steamboat of Clermont successfully moved people from New York City to Albany (a 300-mile trip) in 62 hours in 1807. Later, Cornelius Vanderbilt (1794-1877) revolutionized travel by making ocean voyages faster, more efficient, and less expensive, eventually moving people from New York City to California.

The Industrial Revolution changed the way families lived and worked. Before the Industrial Revolution, most families worked together on a farm, but after, each person in the family went to a factory to work. In the North, cities grew to incredible size by 1860, with places like New York City numbering 813,669, Philadelphia 565,529, Brooklyn 266,661, and Baltimore 212,418. The largest southern city was New Orleans with 168,675.

Many people falsely glamorize life on a farm, but the Industrial Revolution created the opportunity for many to leave the harsh conditions of farm life and go to the city. At the young age of 5 or 6, kids would wake up before sunrise to toil on the family farm. By the age of 10, boys and girls on the farm were expected to work the same hours as adults, meaning "sunup to sundown." The Industrial Revolution made it possible for women to have greater economic opportunities. On the farm, women could only do work involving the family's everyday needs, such as cooking, cleaning, and sewing clothing. In cities, there were a wider variety of jobs girls and women could have.

Because of the Industrial Revolution and the North's laws against slavery, the North led the South in many important areas. Most immigrants to the U.S.A. in the 1800s went to the North, because they could not compete against the slaves for jobs in the South. This led to a population boom in the North and a population dearth in the South. By 1860, there were wide percentage differences between the North and South in many areas.

1860	**NORTH**	**SOUTH**
Population	71%	29%
Railroad Mileage	72%	28%
Iron/Steel Production	92%	8%
Wealth	75%	25%
Value of Imports	68%	32%
Factories	85%	15%
Large Farms	16%	84%

Crime in cities was one element of life in the North that was not found in the South. By the 1860s, the homicide rate of New York City had grown to equal that of New York City in the year 2000! Uniformed policemen made their first debut in America. One policemen referred to a dangerous section of New York City as Hell, but his colleague responded by saying it was hotter than Hell and was in fact "Hell's Kitchen." Other dangerous areas were called the Bowery, Rag Picker's Row, Mulligan Alley, Satan's Circus, and Cockroach Row. In 1860, New York City had 30,000 unsupervised orphans, 15,000 beggars, and widespread prostitution.

Gangs ran the streets of New York and were often organized by ethnic groups, many emerging from the Five Points neighborhood. One gang, the Forty Thieves, had a daily quota for each gang member to steal. The Bowery Boys would dress elegantly, but would beat up and terrorize those who voted against their favored politicians. The Dead Rabbits gang excelled at robbery, picking pockets, and fighting. One of their fights against the Bowery Boys resulted in the murder of 12 people. One female Dead Rabbit, nicknamed "Hell-Cat Maggie," reportedly filed her teeth to points and wore brass fingernails into battle. The Daybreak Boys snuck onto ships on the East River, stealing the cargo, and often murdering a watchman. To join the Daybreak Boys, it was rumored that a prospective gang member had to kill someone.

Chapter 52

Life in the West

In the United States, the West was a changing geographical phenomenon. Life in the West, and the hope and stories the West provided for the rest of the country, defined what America was, both for Americans and foreigners. Nowhere in the world was there so much land, such beautiful and open spaces, and such a challenging natural world to overcome. After the American Revolution ended in 1783, the West was the area beyond the Appalachian Mountains. The purchase of the Louisiana Territory (1803) and the Lewis and Clark Expedition expanded the West across the Great Plains. The Mexican-American War (1846-1848) and the Oregon Treaty (1848) opened the West all the way to the Pacific Ocean.

In the late 1700s and first part of the 1800s, fur trappers, mountain men, and explorers set bravely out into the frontier. The frontier was the territory beyond civilization. Often venturing out on their own, fur trappers would hunt for animals with valuable pelts, such as beaver, fox, deer, and bear. The fur trappers would take the beaver pelts to market and trade them for supplies.

After the Lewis and Clark Expedition (1804-1806) opened up the West, American explorers, fur trappers, and then pioneer families moved westward in ever increasing numbers. With the conclusion of the Mexican-American War and the Oregon Treaty, the United States spanned the continent within a century of its founding. Thomas Jefferson had believed it would take 1,000 years for America to expand to the Pacific Ocean.

Jedediah Strong Smith (1799-1831) was one of the most famous mountain men. Mountain men were Americans, or Frenchmen from Canada, who ventured west before the pioneer families, trapping fur animals, making maps, and befriending and marrying Indians. Smith was a clerk, frontiersman, hunter, trapper, author, cartographer, and explorer. It is said that he travelled on horse with a rifle in one hand and a Bible in the other. Smith was the first American to cross the Sierra Nevada Mountains and the Great Basin Desert. In 1831 Smith was killed by Comanche Indians.

Davy Crockett (1786-1836) was both real and an American legend. He was a folk hero, frontiersman, soldier, and politician. Crockett grew up in Tennessee, where he became well-known for hunting and storytelling. He volunteered and fought the Creek Indians under General Andrew Jackson. Davy had three children with his wife Polly before she died and he remarried. Stories, or "tall tales," spread and Americans learned that Davy could "grin a bar to death" (kill a bear with his grin), was half-alligator and half-horse (he was tough and fast), and was honest. Crockett's popularity grew because of his true and legendary exploits.

Crockett's public life began as a soldier, but later he became a politician. He was a judge, a state representative, and then a representative in the U.S. Congress. In 1830, Crockett was the only Tennessee representative to vote against the President Jackson-approved Indian Removal Act. His vote was unpopular in Tennessee, and Crockett lost in the next election. He won one more election, and then lost his last one. In 1836, newspapers published a quote attributed to Crockett at that time, "I told the people of my district that I would serve them as faithfully as I had done; but if not, they might go to hell, and I would go to Texas."

Crockett did go to Texas, and it was there he died. Earlier, in the U.S., Crockett had stated that if Jackson's hand-picked successor, Martin Van Buren, won the election, than he would go to Texas. After Van Buren won, Crockett left the country for good, and arrived during the Texas War for Independence. Crockett chose to help the Texans at the Alamo, a small mission in southern Texas. Texans were trying to break away from Mexico, and were using the Alamo as a fort. As reported in greater detail earlier in this book, the Mexicans took the Alamo, and slaughtered all of the Texans, but not before suffering great losses. There is some debate how Crockett died. One report states that his body was found in the middle of 16 dead Mexican soldiers. Another states that he surrendered, and then was bayoneted by a large group of soldiers under the direction of Santa Anna. A third says that Crockett was killed by a Mexican firing squad the morning after the battle ended. Crockett is remembered as an honest, tough, and valiant American and is a symbol of the American West.

After the mountain men and explorers, pioneer families moved west, often in Conestoga Wagons. Conestoga Wagons were built to hold all of a family's possessions, and made to traverse thousands of miles. Many pioneer families followed the Oregon Trail, as described earlier in this book. Other settlers travelled southwest to Utah and to central and southern California. These pioneers made the greatest change on the continent, establishing families, communities, and bringing American culture permanently to the West.

CHAPTER 53

IMMIGRATION

During the first half of the 1800s, and even through the Civil War, millions of people throughout the world left their homelands and risked their lives to make the North and West of America their new home. The immigrants chose the United States of America and primarily the North and West over the South due to the North's and West's inexpensive land, economic opportunities, small government, capitalism, and the idea that in America, all men are created equal. In Canada, Mexico, South America, and in the South of the U.S.A., capitalism and freedom were limited.

Americans continued to force one immigrant group, the slave, to come to America until the importation of slavery was abolished in 1807. At that point, the United States slave population was so large that it no longer mattered. Slaves are the only immigrant group to America that did not achieve gains in society, because they were not allowed their freedom in the South.

Americans were united by ideas, not by national ethnic group or class. One of America's mottos, E Pluribus Unum, means "From many, we are one." This idea means that the U.S.A. is a country made up of people from all over the world, and not just the home of people from England and France. People came to America because of the American ideals of freedom and because in America, a person could have equal rights with everyone. In most other countries in the 1800s, a person's nationality was the most important thing in determining his allegiance. A French immigrant would not have been welcome in countries other than the U.S., for example. And, in most other countries, individuals had rights that depended on their class. If someone was not a nobleman, he could not own land or have political liberties. America's unique ideas attracted immigrants.

Immigrants also came to America for economic opportunities. Nowhere in the world but America was there inexpensive land and laws that treated all citizens the same. Immigrants saw that in the U.S.A., a person could own his own small farm and support a family. In most countries of the world, only the nobility could own land. Also, especially in Northern cities, Americans needed immigrants to work in the new factories. The Industrial Revolution allowed for amazing economic opportunities for men and women, and many jobs did not require skills. Immigrants were excited to get off a boat and land a job within days. Although they struggled at first, immigrants and their children reaped long-term benefits.

Immigrants to America between 1800 and 1860 mainly came from northwestern Europe and their number increased with each decade. At the turn of the century, most immigrants came from Great Britain (including Scotland and Northern Ireland) and France. By the 1840s, Germans, Irish, and Scandinavians came in larger numbers.

DECADE	NUMBER OF IMMIGRANTS TO THE U.S.A.
1820's	143,439
1830's	599,125
1840's	1,713,251
1850's	2,598,214

Starting in the 1840s, one of the largest immigrant groups to America was the Irish. In Ireland, a new fungus caused potatoes to rot in the fields. Because most Irish were poor and worked on potato farms owned by the English, and there was practically no other food in Ireland, approximately one million (out of 8 million) Irish died of starvation or disease from 1845 to 1849. Many people also believe that the English refused to send help to the Irish. The Potato Famine of the 1840s pushed nearly 2 million Irish to move to America in the 1840s and 1850s.

In America, the Irish faced great discrimination, but eventually were accepted as Americans. The Irish had been hated by the English in Great Britain, and in America, the English-Americans continued the resentment. The Irish were Catholic, and America was primarily a Protestant Christian nation. In the 1800s, people were very sensitive of the differences between the Protestant Christian and Catholic Christian faiths, and Protestant Americans did not immediately accept the Catholic Irish. Irish Catholic churches were bombed, and Irish were not hired in many jobs.

The Irish settled primarily in Northern cities. Like all immigrants, the first generation worked in menial jobs. The second generation took jobs in the public world, especially in fire departments and police departments. The Irish tended to vote Democratic, and political corruption seemed to follow the Irish-American population. In Great Britain, the Irish had little or no respect for the official government, and in America, it was perhaps simpler for Irish-Americans to be open to fraud. Tammany Hall, a Democratic political machine in New York City, helped the Irish and used illegal and unethical tactics to maintain power throughout much of the second half of the 1800s.

Germans also came to America in ever-increasing numbers throughout the 1800s, in part because of problems in Europe. In Europe, Germans and the inhabitants of the Austro-Hungarian Empire lived in a monarchical system, where the common person had few of the liberties available in America. Land was expensive or impossible to buy. The government did not allow political liberties. Then, in 1848, many Europeans rose up to challenge the power of the kings. European kings crushed the revolutions of 1848, and common Europeans saw it was nearly impossible to achieve the rights that Americans enjoyed.

In the 1850s, 951,000 Germans came to America. German immigrants were skilled laborers, and had experience in steel making, mechanics, making musical instruments, and brewing. The American brewery companies Schlitz, Pabst, and Budweiser were founded by German-Americans. German immigrants created the famous Kentucky long rifle, the Conestoga

Wagon, the first wire cable suspension bridge (to Brooklyn), and the Heinz food company. A large percentage of Germans moved to U.S. farmland, settling the Appalachian Valley, the Midwest, and near cities such as Cincinnati, Milwaukee, and St. Louis. Germans were the largest immigrant group to America in the 1800s.

UNIT X

THE SLAVERY CRISIS BECOMES VIOLENT, 1848-1860

INTRODUCTION

In 1848, America was a country with two vastly different stories. One was a story of liberty, of the freest country on Earth, a success story of capitalism, free markets and freedom of religion, in a place that attracted millions of immigrants from around the world. The other story was about a country of privilege, where the most important thing in life was the circumstance of your birth, where 5-6 million white people enslaved over 3 million black people, and where an elite group made decisions for all of society. Thomas Jefferson wrote in the Declaration of Independence the ideal of America, that "all men are created equal." However, it was only in the free North where the law represented this ideal. In 1858, Abraham Lincoln stated, "A house divided against itself cannot stand. I believe this government cannot endure permanently half slave and half free. I do not expect the Union to be dissolved – I do not expect the house to fall – but I do expect that it will cease to be divided." Lincoln's expectations proved to be true.

Chapter 54

Political Instability and the End of Westward Expansion

From 1837 to 1860, there was great instability in the American presidency as no president served two terms. One president lost his reelection battle, two died in office, two chose not to run for reelection, and three were not renominated to run for office. In 22 years, there were eight Presidents. Americans were unhappy with their leaders, and leaders tried to stay away from the topic of slavery altogether.

In 1848, America won the Mexican Cession in the Mexican-American War (1846-1848), and the U.S.A. completed its northern boundary with Great Britain in the Northwest with the Oregon Treaty (1848). Many Americans rejoiced, because the country now spanned "from sea to shining sea." However, the addition of new lands brought with it the question about the expansion of slavery. Would the new lands in the Southwest and the Oregon Territory be slave or free? Nobody knew. The Missouri Compromise of 1820 had decided the slavery issue only as it applied to the Louisiana Territory. Anti-slavery advocate Ralph Waldo Emerson wrote that taking the Mexican Cession was like taking arsenic – it would poison the country to death. Emerson was correct. The problem of deciding what the new lands would be – slave or free – was one of the main causes of the Civil War.

The Election of 1848 and a Values-Free Policy

"I am personally against it, but who am I to decide for others?"
"I think it is immoral, but who am I to tell another how to live?"
"It's not up to me to decide how others should live their lives."

These arguments were made by Northern politicians regarding the issue of slavery. Hoping to attract votes of slaveholders, these politicians would argue that they did not think their personal morality should dictate law for everyone.

Having a values-free political stand, or a values-free education, or a values-free country, is impossible. The "live and let live" philosophy of these Northern politicians meant that slavery could continue and expand. Letting someone else enslave another is condoning violence. As historians Michael Allen and Larry Schweikart write, "not to call evil, evil, is to call it good."

The Democratic candidate for president in 1848, Lewis Cass of Michigan, introduced the idea of "popular sovereignty." Popular sovereignty meant that each state would vote if it would be a free or a slave state. Candidate Cass, supported by Stephen Douglas of Illinois, believed this political solution gave the Democrats the best answer on the hot button issue of slavery. Cass and Douglas thought they could argue that although they believed slavery was immoral, they did not feel that they should make a moral decision for others. Popular sovereignty took the decision out of their hands, and was essentially sold as a "values-free" stance.

The other major political party, the Whigs, chose Zachary "Old Rough-and-Ready" Taylor as its presidential candidate. Taylor was a hero of the Mexican-American War, and his campaign relied mainly on his military experience and accomplishments. Taylor was a Southerner and owned plantations in Louisiana, Kentucky, and Mississippi. He obviously was for slavery and appealed to some Southerners.

The founder of the Democratic Party, Martin Van Buren, had since left and started a new party, the Free Soil Party. Van Buren now believed that slavery needed to be eradicated. The Free Soil Party stood for "Free Soil, Free Speech, Free Labor, and Free Men." In the voting, the Free Soil Party came in third.

Zachary Taylor won the election, and the next four years were filled with political rancor over slavery. After the election, slave states met at a special convention and discussed leaving the Union. Taylor said that he would hang anyone who tried to disrupt the Union by force or by conspiracy. Within a little over a year, Taylor caught a stomach illness and died on July 4, 1850. His successor was Millard Fillmore (1850-1853), who was the only president besides the Adamses to have not owned a slave. His presidency was also dominated by the issue of slavery. Though he opposed slavery personally, he was unwilling to stop its expansion.

THE COMPROMISE OF 1850

In 1850, California was ready to be admitted into the United States of America, and this event caused great problems. Would California enter as a free or a slave state? How would the other new territories in the Southwest be admitted? Americans tried to answer these two questions so both the pro-slavery South and the anti-slavery North would be happy. Ultimately, an answer that pleased both could not be found, which eventually led to the Civil War.

In the Mexican-American War (1846-48), the U.S.A. took an area that would later become California, Nevada, Utah, Arizona, New Mexico, and parts of Colorado and Wyoming. In 1848, America also gained the future states of Oregon, Washington, Idaho, and parts of Wyoming and Montana through the Oregon Treaty. Polk had won the 1844 election promising a free Oregon and slavery in Texas. Americans believed it might be ten or twenty years before they would need to answer the question about slavery in the other new territories. However, within two years, the problem of slavery in the new territories came to a head. In 1848, John Marshall discovered gold at Sutter's Mill, east of Sacramento, and within a year, over 100,000 '49ers rushed into California to find gold. Soon, California wanted to be admitted as a state.

California was admitted into the United States of America as a part of five separate bills called the Compromise of 1850. The Compromise had five points:
1. California was admitted as a free state.
2. Citizens of the future Utah and New Mexico would decide by popular sovereignty if they would be slave or free.

3. The Texas western border was agreed upon.
4. The slave trade was eliminated in Washington, D.C., but slavery itself continued to be legal there.
5. A Fugitive Slave Law forced Northerners to capture and return runaway slaves.

A compromise is meant to make both sides happy enough so that arguing will not continue, however, the Compromise of 1850 brought America closer to war. Popular sovereignty caused great violence, as militants on both sides realized that if they killed enough people on the other side, then when it came time to vote, their side had a better chance of winning the vote. The Fugitive Slave Law forced Northerners who opposed slavery to capture runaway slaves and return them into captivity. The Fugitive Slave Law made Northerners accomplices in the practice of slavery and caused more Northerners to become abolitionists.

Chapter 55

The Decade Preceding the Civil War

During the Civil War, 6 foot-4 inch Abraham Lincoln met 4 foot-11 inch Harriet Beecher Stowe, the author of Uncle Tom's Cabin (1852). One rendition of the meeting quotes Lincoln saying to Stowe, "So this is the little woman that started this big war." Stowe's book is the story of Tom, a Christian slave, and his journey from one slave owner to another. Eventually, Tom is sold "down the river" to an evil slave owner, Simon Legree. Simon Legree attempts to stop Tom from reading his Bible and acting as a Christian. Then, Legree brutally murders Tom. Other slaves try to escape along the Underground Railroad and some make it to safety. Uncle Tom's Cabin is fiction, but became the example of slavery for Northerners. This novel made many Northerners believe that all Southern slave holders were evil, like Simon Legree.

Presidency of Franklin Pierce (1853-1857)

Franklin Pierce was a Northern Democrat who believed popular sovereignty was the best way to resolve the slavery issue in the new western lands. He viewed the abolitionist movement as the greatest threat to the Union. In 1854, he championed and signed the Kansas-Nebraska Act. This act was drafted by Senator Stephen Douglas and declared that when Kansas and Nebraska were ready for statehood, their free people would vote whether or not their state would be free. Pierce vigorously enforced the Fugitive Slave Law.

Bleeding Kansas

Stephen Douglas' Kansas-Nebraska Act was a major cause of open warfare in Kansas from 1854 to 1861. This Act destroyed the Missouri Compromise of 1820, which stated that this area of the Louisiana Territory would be free. Once the law was passed, vigilante groups and "self-defense" associations came to Kansas, looking for a fight. Even congressmen encouraged violence. Using the strongest possible words, pro-slavery Missouri Senator David

Atchison vowed to kill every abolitionist. In 1856, John Brown and his antislavery followers brutally murdered five men and boys in what was called the "Pottawatomie Massacre." By the end of 1856, over 200 people had been murdered in Kansas. A vote in Kansas did take place, but there was so much conflict over the election that Kansas was not allowed to enter as a state at that time.

Violence in Congress

In 1856, abolitionist Massachusetts Senator Charles Sumner gave an impassioned, vitriolic speech against slavery and specifically against Illinois Senator Stephen Douglas and South Carolina Senator Andrew Butler. South Carolina Democratic Congressman Preston Brooks (Butler's nephew) challenged Republican Sumner to a duel, and Sumner refused. Then, immediately after a session of Congress, but still in the Senate chamber, Brooks walked over to Sumner, took his walking cane, and beat Sumner until he was bloody and unconscious. Brooks' cane broke, but he continued to beat Sumner after he was unconscious. Finally, he stopped the beating. Sumner took years to recover his health, and may not have ever completely recovered. Later, the city of Charleston gave Congressman Brooks a new cane inscribed with the words, "Hit him again!" The Senate tried to censure Brooks but failed. Brooks then resigned from office, and was quickly reelected.

Presidency of James Buchanan (1857-1861)

Three political parties competed in the election of 1856. The Whig Party, which originated in the 1830s, had died out, mainly because Whigs refused to address slavery as a moral issue. The Democratic Party candidate James Buchanan argued that slavery should be decided by popular sovereignty. A new party, the Republican Party, strongly opposed the expansion of slavery and viewed slavery as immoral. The American Party was nicknamed the "Know Nothing Party" because its members refused to answer questions involving how the party operated. The American Party was based on dislike of immigrants, especially Irish Catholics. Of the popular vote, Buchanan won 45.3%, Fremont of the Republican Party won 33.1%, and Fillmore of the American Party won 21.5%.

Dred Scott Decision

Just two months after the inauguration of James Buchanan, the Supreme Court ruled in the Dred Scott decision (Dred Scott v. Sandford, 1857) that a "slave was a slave everywhere." The Supreme Court ruled that because a slave was property, the slave owner had the right to take his slave to any territory in the country. This ruling made every territory a potential slave state. Supreme Court Chief Justice Roger B. Taney wrote that blacks were "a subordinate and inferior class of beings [who] had not rights which the white man was bound to respect." The Dred Scott decision completely destroyed 70 years of laws regarding the expansion of slavery, and it demolished a key argument of the Declaration of Independence, that "all men are created equal." It was an unacceptable ruling for anti-slavery Northerners and abolitionists. From this point on, many Northerners believed that Southerners controlled the court system and the presidency, and that the law-making process was corrupt.

John Brown's Raid on Harper's Ferry

On October 18, 1859, abolitionist John Brown and a gang of 17 whites and 5 blacks took over a federal arsenal in Harper's Ferry, Virginia. Brown's goal was to free and arm slaves, and start a race war in the South that would kill all of the slave owners. Brown believed that God was on his side. President Buchanan ordered Colonel Robert E. Lee and his lieutenant, J.E.B. Stuart, to take Marines and defeat Brown. U.S. soldiers killed ten, captured Brown, and quelled the revolt. Brown was tried and hung for treason. The raid on Harper's Ferry caused paranoia in the South, with white Southerners believing all Northerners to be as violent as John Brown. And, although Brown had a family history of lunacy and was most likely crazy, Northerners like Ralph Waldo Emerson called him a "new saint."

CHAPTER 56

ABRAHAM LINCOLN

Abraham Lincoln was the most hated and despised president of all time, yet he is one of America's greatest presidents. During the years before the presidential election of 1860, Lincoln clearly stated that slavery was a morally evil and corrupt institution, and that one day, the country would be either all free or all slave. His clarity on this issue led the South to believe that Lincoln would try to abolish slavery, even though he never stated he would. His election to the presidency in 1860 pushed the first Southern states to secede and form the Confederate States of America. Over the next four years, 1861-1865, Lincoln led the effort to crush the rebellion in the South.

Lincoln's circumstances of youth were common to many Americans. He was born on February 12, 1809, in Kentucky, in a log cabin. His family was part of the Separate Baptist Church, which forbade alcohol, dancing, and slavery. Abraham's dad, Thomas, saw Indians kill his own father. When Abraham was 9, his family moved north to Indiana. Then, Abraham's mom died. About a year later, Thomas remarried to Sarah, called "Sally." Abraham came to love Sally and called her "mother." As a young person, Abraham learned to read and write at an "ABC School" a few weeks per year. In ABC Schools, children in a larger community met at a log cabin and were taught by a private tutor. Lincoln read the Bible, Robinson Crusoe, Decline and Fall of the Roman Empire, Franklin's Autobiography, and law books, whenever he had extra time. At the age of 21, Lincoln moved west to Illinois.

As a boy and young man, Lincoln was known as physically strong and a person of wit. He was 6 feet, 4 inches tall, lanky and wiry. For fun, he would tell stories and wrestle. Lincoln is enshrined in the Wrestling Hall of Fame, and had a 300-1 record. Once, after beating his opponent, Lincoln looked at the crowd and declared, "I'm the big buck of this lick. If any of you want to try it, come on and whet your horns." Nobody took him up on the offer.

Lincoln was a reader, a hard worker, and a person of character whom others respected. He read the few books he had many times, and when possible, he borrowed books from other frontier settlers. While living with his parents, he worked on the family farm all day. Lincoln traveled by flatboat down the Mississippi River in 1828 and 1831, and he later received a patent pertaining to flatboats. In the Black Hawk War, Lincoln was voted militia corporal. When he lived on his own, Lincoln opened a store with his partner, who then embezzled all the money. Lincoln worked to pay off the resulting debt of $1,000 (equal to about $26,000 in 2017). Later he decided to be a lawyer.

Lincoln's understanding of religion changed over time. As a young man, he was skeptical that God and Jesus Christ existed. Later, he believed in Christ, but he still rejected joining a religious denomination. Toward the end of his life, Lincoln was convinced of the truth of the New Testament and was led by his faith. In the election of 1846, he campaigned, "I am not a member of any Christian Church…but I have never denied the truth of the Scriptures." During the Civil War, Lincoln professed a conversion experience to Christianity. Immediately after the Battle of Gettysburg, Lincoln visited the battle scene. He wrote this of what happened:

When I left Springfield I asked the people to pray for me. I was not a Christian. When I buried my son, the severest trial of my life, I was not a Christian. But when I went to Gettysburg and saw the graves of thousands of our soldiers, I then and there consecrated myself to Christ. Yes, I love Jesus. After this, Lincoln prayed every day and read the Bible. To a friend he wrote, "Take all of this book [the Bible] upon reason you can, and the balance on faith, and you will live and die a happier and better man."

Abraham Lincoln married Mary Todd in 1842 and had four boys. Though Lincoln left Mary Todd at the altar during their first wedding attempt, Lincoln called marriage a "profound wonder." His son Edward died at the age of four of thyroid cancer. William died at the age of 12 of typhoid fever. Tad died of pneumonia at the age of 18. Only Robert lived into adulthood, dying in 1926. The boys' deaths were a source of great sadness for the Lincolns.

Neither Mr. nor Mrs. Lincoln was known for physical beauty, but they were known for their character, ideas, and determination. Mary once said of her husband, "Mr. Lincoln is to be president of the United States some day. If I had not thought so, I would not have married him, for you can see he is not pretty."

In 1858, Americans learned a great deal about the thoughts of Abraham Lincoln through the Lincoln-Douglas Debates. Republican Abraham Lincoln was running for an Illinois U.S. Senate seat against the incumbent Democratic Senator Stephen Douglas. Lincoln was relatively unknown in the country, and many believed Douglas would one day be president. Lincoln and Douglas debated seven times, with each debate lasting around three hours. The debates were big events, with bands, food, and whiskey. At the end of each debate, the candidates shook hands, and maintained a cordial, friendly attitude toward each other. There was no questioner or moderator, only the two men on stage, speaking at great length.

At the Lincoln-Douglas Debates, the two candidates expressed greatly different views, especially on slavery. Lincoln spoke strongly against slavery, calling it a moral evil. Lincoln's clear and unequivocal talk on slavery angered Southern Democrats who wanted slavery to expand. Douglas stated that he was personally against slavery, but he favored popular sovereignty, that the decision should be left to the people in the individual states.

At the last debate, Lincoln stated,
> *The real issue is the sentiment on the part of one class that looks upon the institution of slavery as a wrong…The Republican Party look(s) upon it as being a moral, social and political wrong…and one of the methods of treating it as a wrong is to make provision that it shall grow no larger…That is the real issue."* [The black man is] *"entitled to all the natural rights enumerated in the Declaration of Indepen-*

dence, the right to life, liberty, and the pursuit of happiness…In the right to eat the bread, without leave of anybody else, which his own hand earns, he is my equal and the equal of Judge Douglas, and the equal of every living man."

In the Lincoln-Douglas Debates, Lincoln argued that the new Republican Party believed the Southern states opposed the ideals found in the Declaration of Independence. Lincoln saw slavery as a sin, as evil, and as a threat to liberty and equality for all. How Lincoln foresaw ending slavery, however, was through legal means, either by voting or appointing Northern judges who would chip away at slavery in the courts. He wanted to peacefully abolish slavery through law, over time.

Stephen Douglas won the 1858 Senate election against Abraham Lincoln, but Lincoln became a national political figure. All Americans understood that Lincoln and the Republicans saw slavery as morally corrupt, and that over time, they would work to end it. When Lincoln was elected president in 1860, the Southern states believed they had to secede from the Union in order to preserve the Southern culture, which included slavery.

UNIT XI

THE CIVIL WAR

INTRODUCTION

From 1776 to 1861, Americans experienced amazing growth in economics, territory, and technology, as well as great advances in communication and transportation. Immigrants from every part of the world flocked to the United States of America more than to any other country. However, the problem of slavery created two violently opposing views. Over half the country wanted slavery to stop expanding, and many wanted it to immediately end, yet a great number of Southerners felt that owning slaves was their God-given, Constitutionally-guaranteed right. The South believed that if the Republican Lincoln were elected president, he would immediately move to end slavery, either through the law-making process or by appointing Supreme Court justices opposed to slavery. Southerners saw Northerners as hypocritical moralists with no right to take away a citizen's private property. How could someone tell another person how to live? Northerners and a very small number of Southern abolitionists wanted all Americans to enjoy equal rights as soon as possible. These opposing viewpoints were eventually settled on the battlefield, during the Civil War (1861-1865).

The Civil War is America's deadliest, most tragic, and most influential war. Over 620,000 men lost their lives in battle, in captivity, or through disease. Another 476,000 men were wounded, and 400,000 were either captured or missing. As a percentage of society, this would be the equivalent of 6 million dead in 2017. Nearly all eligible, white Southerners served in the war, and almost half were either killed, wounded, captured, or missing during the approximately 10,500 battles of the war. The Civil War is the key pivotal moment in the history of the United States of America. After the war, the country took a different direction in many ways.

CHAPTER 57

THE ELECTION OF 1860

In the 1860 presidential election, the Democratic Party split in two. From 1848 to 1860, the Democratic Party had attempted to ignore the problem of slavery, nominating Southern (except Van Buren) candidates who supported an absolute right of the states to decide the issue of slavery. In this way, pro-slavery Southerners and anti-slavery Northerners could vote for the Democratic candidate. In 1860, however, Southern Democratic delegates demanded that the Democratic Party promote a national law enforcing slavery. The leading Democrat, Stephen Douglas, would not support this demand. Because of this, Northern Democrats supported Douglas, and Southern Democrats supported Vice President John C. Breckenridge, the pro-slavery candidate. The split of the Democratic Party made it easier for the other major party, the Republicans, to win.

Two more candidates ran in the 1860 presidential election: Republican Abraham Lincoln and Constitutional Unionist John Bell, a Tennessee slaveholder. Abraham Lincoln had vigorously argued against slavery in his bid to win the Illinois Senate seat in 1858 and was known across America. The Republican position that slavery was immoral, corrupt, and a paradox to the ideals of the United States of America made it popular in the North but unacceptable in the South. The Constitutional Union Party was supported by former Southern Democrats who were not as strongly pro-slavery as the Southern Democrat John C. Breckenridge.

The election resulted in a stunning victory against slavery and the South, though no candidate won the popular vote.

CANDIDATE	ELECTORAL	STATES VOTE	POPULAR VOTE CARRIED	% OF VOTE
Abraham Lincoln	29%	18	1,865,908	39.8%
Stephen Douglas	28%	1	1,380,202	29.5%
John Breckenridge	8%	11	848,019	18.1%
John Bell	25%	3	590,901	12.6%

Republican Abraham Lincoln, the anti-slavery candidate, won the election, capturing 18 states and a majority of the electoral votes. Republicans also captured a majority in the Senate and the House of Representatives. Stephen Douglas was portrayed (falsely) in the South as a Free Soiler. Douglas and Lincoln together won over 69% of the total vote. Together, Bell and Breckenridge captured fewer than 31% of the vote. Before 1861, a Southern slaveholder had held the presidential office 49 out of 72 years. Twenty of the 35 Supreme Court justices had come from slaveholding states. The 1860 election showed Southerners that Lincoln and Northern future presidential candidates did not need the South to win, and that eventually, the United States of America would move to end slavery. Southerners worried that "black Republicans" would control Supreme Court justices, federal marshals, postmasters, and all federal officers. Lincoln's election was the beginning of the end of the Union of slave and free states.

CHAPTER 58

SECESSION AND THE CONFEDERATE STATES OF AMERICA

Immediately after Abraham Lincoln won the presidential election, South Carolina led seven Southern states to secede and form a new country. Southern state legislatures chose delegates, and these delegates chose secession in this order: South Carolina, Mississippi, Alabama, Georgia, Louisiana, Texas, and Florida. South Carolina called for a Southern states convention, and a constitution was written for the new country, the Confederate States of America (C.S.A.). Not all Southerners wanted to secede, however, and over 100,000 soldiers from the seceding states fought for the Union.

The main reason the Southern states left the Union and the primary reason for the Civil War was slavery and race. The secession document of each Southern state declared that the state was leaving the Union in order to preserve slavery. In the C.S.A. Constitution, the rights of the slave owner over slaves were affirmed. The new C.S.A. federal government subsidized slave owners in the legal enforcement of the institution. Southerners paid taxes that went towards capturing and returning runaway slaves. The poorest of white Southerners had to pay to help capture the escaped slaves of the richest plantation owners. C.S.A. Vice President Alexander H. Stephens stated, "Our new Government is founded…upon the great truth that the negro is not the equal of the white man. That slavery – subordination to the superior race, is his natural and normal condition." C.S.A. President Jefferson Davis stated, "On and after February 22, 1863, all free negroes within the limits of the Southern Confederacy shall be placed on slave status, and be deemed to be chattels, they and their issue forever." Davis also declared that any free blacks taken from free states would also become slaves.

After slavery and race, Southerners pointed to two other reasons for secession: states' rights and the supremacy of cotton. States' rights was the idea that each state had power equal to the central (federal) government. While Southerners claimed to support this idea, the C.S.A. Constitution had fewer checks on federal power than the U.S. Constitution. The C.S.A. had no Supreme Court to check the president and Congress. And, a Southern state could never decide independently of the country to free its slaves. Southern leaders severely limited Southern states' rights. It is ironic that the states in the Union had more power than the states of the C.S.A. As for the supremacy of cotton, Southerners believed that with its cotton production, the South and "King Cotton" could dictate to the world. This turned out to be completely false during the Civil War.

Immediately after declaring itself a new country, the C.S.A. demonized the North and used violence to achieve its means. Northerners were called jailbirds, meddlers, busy bodies, and outlaws. Southerners argued that Lincoln would abolish slavery, though he never claimed he would. Lincoln's main goal was keeping the Union as one, and he said he would defend slave owners' rights to do this. Nevertheless, Southern state troops took over federal post offices, customs houses, arsenals, and the New Orleans mint, along with federal gold and silver. The C.S.A. government ordered all Union forces to relinquish their positions and move to the North.

CHAPTER 59

FORT SUMTER AND THE WAR ON PAPER

On March 4, 1861, Abraham Lincoln was inaugurated, and within six weeks, the Civil War began. In early April, Lincoln ordered that Fort Sumter be resupplied with food. To prevent this, Southern troops bombarded the fort. After 34 hours of attack, Major Robert Anderson surrendered the fort. Union forces were allowed to return safely to the North. Northern journalists reported that Southerners attacked the Union, and Lincoln could rightly claim that the South had started the war.

Unlike former President Buchanan, Lincoln acted swiftly, calling upon Americans to send 75,000 soldiers to suppress the rebellion, and he moved to keep the rest of the slave-holding states within the Union. It is believed Lincoln said something like, "I want God on my side, but I've got to have Kentucky." The upper Southern states of Virginia, Arkansas, North Carolina, and Tennessee joined the C.S.A. But partially because of Lincoln's actions, some slaveholding states remained in the Union. West Virginia seceded from Virginia and stayed with the North, and the slave-holding states of Missouri, Kentucky, and Maryland stayed Union.

On paper, it appears the North should have won the Civil War handily. When someone makes a prediction about a competition or war, the estimate is made based on statistics and the guess is called "on paper." This means that the data appears to favor one side over another. However, it is difficult or impossible to gauge emotions, psychology, and other variables that one cannot count. During the Civil War, the North held the advantage in every measurable factor of the industrial era, but the South held the advantage in many intangibles. Because of this, the war lasted for four years, until 1865, and it remains the bloodiest war in American history.

1860	**NORTH**	**SOUTH**
Population	22 million	9 million *(3.2m of these slave)*
soldiers	2.1 million	800,000
volunteers	c. 2 million	600,000
railroad tracks	20,000 miles	10,000 miles
firearms production ratio	32	1
merchant shipping ratio	14	1
farm acreage ratio	3	1
wheat production	412	1
shoe manufacturing	90%	10%

In the areas that are difficult to count, both the North and South had advantages. Northern society was free and capitalistic, where each person benefitted from his own labor. This freedom enabled Northerners to compete in the marketplace and build a society where each person was motivated and rewarded for his work. Northerners created the Gatling Gun and the Spencer repeating rifle. The Gatling Gun was one of the first rapid-fire weapons and the Spencer repeating rifle allowed the shooter to fire seven shots without reloading. In addition, the freedom and opportunity of the North drew millions of immigrants, and some enlisted in the military upon arriving in the new land. Each individual could freely compete and innovate in Northern society; the North was dynamic and growing economically.

Southern society was based on slavery, race and family, and many Southern leaders argued that their society was the most fair and just. The majority of laborers in Southern society were not allowed to reap the benefits of their hard work. The leaders of the South believed it was their duty and obligation to take care of those under their care, and, like President Jefferson Davis, felt that blacks were better off as slaves and needed to be cared for. Poor whites had little opportunity to advance. Because of these issues, the Southern economy was lethargic and monolithic. Everything was based on cotton, and when cotton failed, the Southern economy failed.

The South's strongest advantages lay in the defensive nature of its position, its seasoned military officers, and its home field advantage. For the Southerners to win, they had to resist the North, and hold out long enough that the North would grow weary of fighting. The North, by contrast, had to conquer and hold a large and diverse enemy territory. Southerners knew every small forest path, and there were no intricate maps available. The South's most celebrated military commander, Robert E. Lee, refused command of the Union Army and successfully led the Army of Northern Virginia. Southern soldiers fought hard, knowing that if they lost, their land would be conquered and their families destroyed.

The North's initial strategy was called the "Anaconda Plan," named after the Anaconda snake of the Amazon region. The Union wanted to control the Mississippi River and blockade the South by controlling the Gulf Coast and the Southern coast. By squeezing the South from the water, the Union wanted to cut all supplies from entering and keep the South from trading with other countries. The Anaconda Plan was not enough to win the war, and thus the Northern plan underwent major adjustments and additions. The North eventually needed to execute two-front, inland assaults and conduct "Hard War." Planners in the North underestimated the difficulty of defeating the South.

The Southern war plan could be described as "King Cotton" and "Attack and Die." The South believed that Great Britain and France needed Southern cotton so much that if the South refused to sell its cotton abroad, these countries would join in fighting the North. The South imposed a cotton embargo against Great Britain and France at the beginning of the war to apply economic pressure. In the end, King Cotton failed miserably as Great Britain and France found other sources for cotton, such as India.

"Attack and Die" is a theory proposed by historians Grady McWhiney and Perry Jamieson. Important to the ideas of Attack and Die is that an agrarian society prides itself on manliness, using frontal attacks with officers in the lead. During the war, 55% of the Southern generals were killed or wounded in battle, Confederate casualty rates outnumbered Northern rates in nearly every battle, and Lee lost 20% in casualties while inflicting a 15% casualty rate on the North. In contrast, Grant suffered an 18% casualty rate but inflicted a 30% rate on the enemy. The Southern belief that to fight a battle well meant to put the troops and leaders in the lead of frontal assaults led to great casualty losses in the South.

President Abraham Lincoln was an amazingly gifted Commander-in-Chief. Lincoln kept the North united in the war effort, maintained a strong economy, and was popular enough to get reelected. Lincoln struggled in finding a General-in-Chief, a supreme commander of all the Union forces, and also a General of the Army of the Potomac, the Union's most important army. From the beginning of the war to the end, Lincoln hired and removed the following from positions of military leadership: Generals Winfield Scott, George McClellan, Henry Halleck, John Pope, Ambrose Burnside and Joe Hooker. Lincoln finally found a winning General-in-Chief in Ulysses S. Grant.

C.S.A. President Jefferson Davis failed in his role as Commander-in-Chief. Unlike Lincoln, Davis held the position of General-in-Chief, until with only a few months left in the war he named Robert E. Lee to this position. Davis had difficulty uniting the various Southern armies, led the Southern economy into the ground, and after Lee surrendered, Davis attempted to lead a Southern guerilla war, but no Southerner followed his lead.

Toward the end of the war, the North implemented what historian James MacPherson describes as "Hard War." Despite great casualties, the North assaulted the South continuously, mobilized the public, destroyed Southern cities, simultaneously attacked on at least two major fronts, and created mass havoc on civilian life, without slaughtering all citizens. Hard War was one major reason the Union defeated the South in the Civil War.

Chapter 60

Bull Run and the Beginning of the War

The first real battle of the war was the Battle of Bull Run on July 16, 1861. Because Virginia was the largest, strongest, and most historically significant state in the South, the capital of the C.S.A. was Richmond, which was also only 100 miles from Washington, D.C., the Union capital and headquarters for all Northern soldiers. Not willing to wait for the Anaconda Plan to work, General McDowell wanted to march soldiers south, win a battle, and walk into Richmond to end the war. 36,000 Union soldiers met 20,000 Confederates at Bull Run, a meandering stream. During the battle, an additional 12,000 Confederate forces under "Stonewall" Jackson joined the fight. Amazingly, hundreds of over-confident spectators came with picnic lunches and blankets to watch the battle.

Southerners won a convincing victory at the Battle of Bull Run. After it became evident the Northerners were losing, thousands of Northern soldiers rid themselves of everything that slowed themselves down, including bags, guns, and ammunition, and literally ran the 26 miles back to Washington, D.C. This was quite the opposite of the legendary Marathon run.
After the battle, the Northern loss spurred Lincoln and Congress to reassess the situation. As a result, they:

1. Reinforced Washington, D.C., to protect it from attack.
2. Passed the Crittenden-Johnson Resolution, which declared war to "defend and maintain the supremacy of the Constitution, and to preserve the Union with all the dignity, equality, and rights of the several States unimpaired."
3. Replaced McDowell with General George B. McClellan as Commander of the Army of the Potomac, and named McClellan as General-in-Chief.

These three moves greatly enhanced the North's chances of success. Washington, D.C., though close to the Southern capital of Richmond, became an impregnable fortress. The Crittenden-Johnson Resolution reassured Northern slave owners that the Union would not free their slaves. This encouraged the key border states of Maryland, Delaware, Kentucky, and Missouri to not break away from the United States

The Union slowly began a "two-front" war in the East and West. In the East, the first year of the war did not go well for the North. General McClellan was an excellent trainer of troops, but was too cautious, demanding ten times the number of soldiers and equipment as the South had before he would fight. Impatient with McClellan, Lincoln issued President's General War Order No. 1 in January 1862, which was to advance. McClellan slowly invaded Virginia, engaging General Lee at the Battles of Seven Pines, Mechanicsville, Gaines' Mill, Frayser's Farm, Malvern Hill, and in other battles. Even after McClellan appeared victorious in one or a few of these battles, he never advanced on Richmond.

Lincoln then replaced McClellan with General John Pope as Commander of the Army of the Potomac. Pope had bragged to Congress that had he been in charge, the war would already be over. Pope then lost to Lee at the Second Battle of Bull Run. However, in each of the battles that Lee fought, the South lost many troops, losing over 13% of the total fighting force. Though the South was winning the battles, it was also losing the men needed to continue fighting.

War on the Atlantic Ocean

While the war was going poorly for the Union in the East, on the Atlantic Ocean the Union was succeeding. One key to the Anaconda Plan was to shut off the trade of the South by blockading all Southern ports. The North succeeded in this effort. The South had little ship building experience, and the great majority of ships' crews remained loyal to the North. Southerners were unable to trade with other countries, and the longer the war raged, the fewer supplies, including guns, blankets, boots, and even food, the South had. By the end of the war, Southern soldiers were hungry, lacked basic clothing, boots and blankets, and did not have enough ammunition.

The Confederates captured the U.S. ship Merrimack, renamed her Virginia, and fitted her with iron plating that was able to repel cannon balls. However, the Union built the Monitor, another ironclad ship. On March 8, 1862, the first ironclad battle in history, known as Monitor vs. Merrimack, ended in a draw. Both ships were unable to fight for the rest of the war, but the future of global naval warfare changed forever on that day.

CHAPTER 61

GROWTH OF GOVERNMENT

To win the war against the South, the United States government grew at an unprecedented rate in power, budget, taxes, and personnel. In 1850, the federal budget was 2% of Gross National Product (GNP). By 1865, it was 15%. In 1850, there were 383 clerks in the Treasury. In 1865, there were 2,000. Before the war, the average citizen felt the presence of the federal government only in the Post Office. After the war, in the South, the federal government was everywhere. Lincoln grew the government because a larger government was needed to defeat the South and preserve the Union. However, much of the increased spending was not related to the war effort, but was pork-barrel legislation.

(Pork-barrel legislation is when Congress spends in order to win votes. Congress pays for projects, giving potential voters money, and thus encouraging these voters to choose the congressman who gave them a salary. A farmer has a pork barrel as a way of storing extra meat that is not essential, but something of a luxury.)

To raise funds to pay the increasing expenses, the federal government passed the National Banking Acts (1863 and 1864), monopolized money, and Secretary of the Treasury Salmon P. Chase created financial instruments and methods that forever altered how government acted in the market. Congress taxed income that was over $300/year, raised tariffs, expanded land sales, sold bonds, and instituted paper money printed in green, nicknamed greenbacks. Chase's friend Jay Cooke sold war bonds, raising $400 million by 1863 and earning him $1 million in commissions.

The National Banking Acts of 1863 and 1864 created a national banking system. In order for banks to get their charters, they had to purchase government bonds. Congress then added a 10% tax on money issued by state banks, thus making the federal banks more profitable. Over time, many state and private banks died. By 1865, there were 1,650 federally chartered banks. Before 1865, the U.S. had the fastest growing economy in the world, and the competition in money was a part of this growth. These National Banking Acts established a federal monopoly over money and changed forever what had been an essential part of the free market system of America.

In contrast to the Union, the Confederate government became a leviathan (a totalitarian state with a vast bureaucracy). In 1862, the C.S.A. confiscated all railroads, steam vessels and telegraph lines. The C.S.A. forced employees of private firms to work for the government. In 1863, though Southern forces were starving in the field, the C.S.A. employed over 70,000 people. Although many argue the real reason the South fought for independence was states' rights, the Confederate government attempted to destroy the power of the Southern states, and infringed upon the individual rights of Southerners. In many ways, the C.S.A. government was socialist and totalitarian.

CHAPTER 62

THE EMANCIPATION PROCLAMATION

One of President Lincoln's actions that proves he was a master statesman, politician, war leader, and moral leader, was the Emancipation Proclamation, issued September 22, 1862, and taking effect January 1, 1863. The Emancipation Proclamation is one of the least understood of Lincoln's actions. He announced it after the Northern victory at Antietam, and it freed the slaves in the rebelling states with consequences that reached much farther than the words stated.

General Robert E. Lee had an undefeated battle record, but, by the fall of 1862, he saw that he needed to bring the war to the North in order to end it. He invaded Maryland at Leesburg. At about this time, a Union soldier took three cigars off of a fallen Rebel soldier. Wrapped inside the cigars were Lee's battle plan instructions that he had secretly sent to his commanders in the field. McClellan then said, "Here is a paper with which if I cannot whip Bobbie Lee, I will be willing to go home."

The Battle of Antietam took place on September 17, 1862, and was a Union success. 85,000 Union soldiers beat 35,000 Confederate soldiers. Lee lost 22% of his men, and on both sides, a total of 24,000 men were killed or wounded on that one day of fighting. However, General McClellan failed to pursue Lee back into Virginia, which allowed Lee's army to escape and fight another day. Because of this, Lincoln replaced McClellan with General Ambrose Burnside as Commander of the Army of the Potomac.

After the victory, Lincoln issued the Emancipation Proclamation, which freed all slaves in the rebelling states. Lincoln explained that slavery was morally unacceptable and made the Union a contradiction. How could a country based on the idea that all men are created equal have slavery? Slavery presented a legal paradox. How could a country based on private property not allow all men the right to their own freedom? However, Lincoln's

Proclamation did not free the slaves in the parts of the Confederacy that were already occupied by Union troops, or in the slave states that fought with the Union. His Emancipation Proclamation was not a complete victory against slavery, but it was a beginning.

The Emancipation Proclamation weakened the Southern war effort in many ways. Slaves in the South were more likely to sabotage war efforts, realizing that a Northern victory would give them freedom. Economically, it threw the South into chaos, as its economy was based on the valuation of slaves. Internationally, the Proclamation meant that Britain and France would never support the South in war, as both countries strongly opposed slavery. The South appeared to be fighting only for slavery, not for states' rights. Eventually, 179,000 black soldiers and 18,000 black sailors fought for the North, representing 9% of the Union force.

CHAPTER 63

HARD WAR

From December 1862 through July 1863, Southern troops scored great victories before losing the most consequential battle of the Civil War. The Union lost the Battles of Fredericksburg and Chancellorsville, but then won the Battle of Gettysburg. However, the Commander of the Army of the Potomac failed to take advantage of the Union victory at Gettysburg to completely defeat the Southern forces. Because of this, the South lived on to fight for nearly two more years. Lincoln replaced his top general a number of times in 1863.

In the East, at the Battle of Fredericksburg, December 11-15, 1862, 78,000 Southern troops defeated 122,000 Northerners. General Burnside had ordered boats to ferry soldiers across the Rappahannock River, but the boats and their transport were delayed. This allowed the Southerners led by General Lee to choose the best defensive positions and dig in. Under a hail of gun and cannon fire, General Burnside directed Union forces to cross the Rappahannock River and occupy the city. Then, Burnside ordered 14 suicidal frontal assaults across an open field straight into the heavily fortified Southern forces. Burnside suffered the worst defeat ever for the U.S. Army. The North lost 12,653 men to the South's 4,201. After the battle, even Southern generals were aghast at the slaughter.

Lincoln then replaced Burnside with General Joe Hooker. At the Battle of Chancellorsville, April 30 to May 6, 1863, Hooker pitted his 133,000 soldiers against Lee's 60,000 troops. Taking a huge risk, Lee divided his smaller army, which caught the North off guard, and won the battle. The only thing that saved the entire Northern army from defeat was the sunset and nightfall.

After the battle, Confederate General "Stonewall" Jackson was accidentally shot and injured by one of his own Southern soldiers. Jackson could no longer fight, and lost his left arm as well. Learning of the amputation, Lee said, "Jackson has lost his left arm, but I have lost my right." In recovery, Jackson caught pneumonia and died. The "victory" at Chancellorsville also cost Lee 20% of his men. The more the North engaged Lee, regardless of loss or victory, the closer the North moved to winning the war.

The South suffered its most consequential defeat of the war in the East at the Battle of Gettysburg, July 1-3, 1863. After the Union debacle at Chancellorsville, Lincoln replaced General Hooker with General Meade as the Commander of the Army of the Potomac. General Lee, though victorious in numerous major battles, was losing men and wanted to bring the war to an end. Lee again invaded the North, hoping to score a major victory, then march on Washington, D.C., and force the Union to surrender. Lee's 75,000 soldiers met Meade's 104,000 soldiers at the town of Gettysburg, Pennsylvania.

In three days of fighting, Meade's forces delivered a crushing and devastating blow to Lee's Army of Northern Virginia. This battle is called the high water mark of the Confederacy, because after this loss the South was never again so close to winning the Civil War. In a battle that has been retold in fiction, non-fiction, in plays, and in movies, the Northern forces gained the upper ground and defended their superior positions on the first two days of fighting. On the third day, the Union forces crushed the Confederate troops.

Two instances of the fighting at Gettysburg demonstrate that combatants on both sides were willing to make the ultimate sacrifice for their cause. On the second day, Maine Colonel Joshua Chamberlain, after leading his unit in furious fighting all day and running out of ammunition, realized that many of his men had no bullets. Instead of surrendering, he led a daring and successful bayonet charge. The Confederate soldiers, also exhausted and running out of ammunition, surrendered. On the third day, General Lee ordered General Pickett to take his army of 15,000 men, march them across a mile-long grass field, and assault the fortified Northern positions. The march of Pickett's men has been called "Pickett's Charge." General Longstreet was strongly against the idea and warned, "General Lee, there never was a body of fifteen thousand men who could make that attack successfully." As the Southerners marched, Northern forces destroyed them with cannon and rifle fire. Virginia General Lewis Armistead reached the stone wall, put his hat atop his sword, and yelled, "Give them the cold steel!" He was killed. The meeting of Northern and Southern lines lasted only minutes, with the North delivering a fateful blow to the Southern war effort. Less than half of the 15,000 men straggled back to the Southern line, with the vengeful Northerners shouting, "Fredericksburg, Fredericksburg!" At the Battle of Gettysburg, the Confederates lost 22,638 and the Union lost 17,684.

Meade could have moved to finish off General Lee and the Army of Northern Virginia, but he did not. Immediately after the battle, Lee could not escape because storms had raised the Potomac River to dangerous levels. However, Meade did not attack and that gave Lee's army time to limp away. Learning of Lee's escape, Lincoln cried. From this point onward, however, General Lee's war effort was limited to escaping complete destruction by the North. Months after the Battle of Gettysburg, on November 19, 1863, Abraham Lincoln travelled to the site of the conflict to dedicate a cemetery, and gave a speech known as the Gettysburg Address. In the speech, Lincoln expressed the ideals on which the United States of America was founded and the reasons the Union had to remain together. He said:

> *Four score and seven years ago our fathers brought forth on this continent, a new nation, conceived in Liberty, and dedicated to the proposition that all men are created equal.*
>
> *Now we are engaged in a great civil war, testing whether that nation, or any nation so conceived and so dedicated, can long endure. We are met on a great battle-field of that war. We have come to dedicate a portion of that field, as a final resting place for those who here gave their lives that that nation might live. It is altogether fitting and proper that we should do this.*

But, in a larger sense, we can not dedicate – we can not consecrate – we can not hallow – this ground. The brave men, living and dead, who struggled here, have consecrated it, far above our poor power to add or detract. The world will little note, nor long remember what we say here, but it can never forget what they did here. It is for us the living, rather, to be dedicated here to the unfinished work which they who fought here have thus far so nobly advanced. It is rather for us to be here dedicated to the great task remaining before us – that from these honored dead we take increased devotion to that cause for which they gave the last full measure of devotion – that we here highly resolve that these dead shall not have died in vain – that this nation, under God, shall have a new birth of freedom – and that government of the people, by the people, for the people, shall not perish from the earth.

Lincoln's short and powerful speech captured the founding principles of America, honored those fighting for the continuation of a free government, and challenged citizens to live up to those ideals. He reminded Americans of the great sacrifice so many citizens had given in the war and rallied others to continue to fight for liberty. He encouraged Americans to be inspired by those who died fighting at the Battle of Gettysburg, and challenged everyone to give all they had to ensure "that government of the people, by the people, for the people, shall not perish from the earth."

In the war on land in the West, President Lincoln had found the commander who would take the bloody fight to the enemy, relentlessly attacking until the goal was accomplished. Ulysses S. Grant's successes on the western battlefields gave the Union what it needed, a man who would win despite great cost. Grant captured Fort Henry (1862) and Fort Donelson (1862) on the Tennessee and Cumberland Rivers. He won the Battle of Shiloh (1862) in Tennessee, and defeated the South at Vicksburg, Mississippi (1863) by starving the townspeople through a seven-month siege of this crucial Mississippi River town. Later, Grant said, "The fate of the Confederacy was sealed when

Vicksburg fell." Lincoln told his advisers, days before Vicksburg fell, "Grant is my man, and I am his for the rest of the war." Also in early July, Union General Meade defeated Lee at Gettysburg. The tide had turned in these pivotal days of July 1863, decidedly in favor of the Union.

Grant's victories came at the cost of immense numbers of casualties. To win a Civil War battle required enormous effort and determination, and the commander could not hesitate to demand great sacrifices from his soldiers. Grant demanded "unconditional and immediate surrender" from his enemies, and earned the nickname "Unconditional Surrender Grant." After the victory at Shiloh, Grant said he could "walk across the clearing in any direction stepping on dead bodies without a foot touching the ground."

CHAPTER 64

UNCONDITIONAL SURRENDER GRANT AND LINCOLN'S REELECTION

In 1864, both the outcome of the Civil War and the reelection of Abraham Lincoln were decided. Of course, both the North and Lincoln eventually won, and the United States remained united, but in early 1864, these outcomes were in great doubt.

Surprisingly, Abraham Lincoln was the most reviled president in the history of the United States. No other president experienced half the country seceding after his election. No other president was blamed by so many for a war that killed 620,000 and wounded over 800,000. And no other president's assassination produced so much joy. Dislike of Lincoln during the war endangered his reelection. If Lincoln had lost the 1864 election, it is possible the Union would have quit the war and the Confederacy would have succeeded.

In early 1864, it looked likely that Lincoln would lose the national election in November. Although the North had won a resounding victory at Gettysburg in July of 1863, there still was no popular sentiment that winning the war was inevitable. General Grant had achieved successes in the war in the West, and Democrats were trying to get him to run for president. General Grant and another successful Union general, General Sherman, did not like Lincoln. Radical Republicans wanted all slaves freed immediately. War Democrats wanted to win the war but keep slavery intact.

Many and much worked against Lincoln's reelection. Copperheads were Northern Democrats who formed secret societies to promote Confederate successes. They stole supplies, destroyed bridges, and issued pro-Southern rulings from the judicial bench. Radical Republicans supported John Fremont as their presidential candidate. Democrats chose General McClellan as their candidate. To supply the army with soldiers, both sides started the first conscription (military draft) in American history. Believing they were unfairly chosen for war, 50,000 Irish immigrants rioted in New York City, destroying $1.5 million of property, and approximately 120 people were killed in the uproar. Even Lincoln thought he would lose to McClellan or Fremont.

In March 1864, Lincoln changed the North's General-in-Chief again, replacing Meade with Ulysses S. Grant. Unlike his predecessors, Grant did not stall but continually attacked. Grant directed the army to destroy anything in the South that would support its war effort, which meant burning and destroying cottages, warehouses, food, animals, and supplies.

The North scored major victories that directly aided the reelection of Lincoln in 1864. Grant inflicted tens of thousands of Confederate casualties in a series of Virginia battles. Admiral David Farragut captured Mobile Bay, Alabama, on August 5. In addition, General Phillip Sheridan destroyed Southern forces in the Shenandoah Valley of Virginia. With victory in sight, Americans reelected Abraham Lincoln.

After Lincoln's election, the North continued the savage fight. General William Tecumseh Sherman's "march to the sea" destroyed Atlanta and burned a path some claim was 60 miles wide to the coast at Savannah. Sherman's men lived off the land and obliterated Georgia's ability to fight. Grant believed that the only way the South would surrender was if the North destroyed everything that was productive in the Confederacy.

Chapter 65

The End of the War and Lincoln's Assassination

The final step of the war was Grant's encircling of Lee's starving Army of Northern Virginia. Grant laid siege to and forced the city of Petersburg, Virginia, to surrender. There was nowhere for the Army of Northern Virginia to go, so the only option for Lee was to give up. On April 9, 1865, General Grant accepted General Lee's surrender at Appomattox, Virginia. Over the next few months, as word spread slowly, the remaining Southern armies surrendered.

Lee's surrender took place in the parlor of a private home, and the terms of the surrender set the tone for the peace that followed. Lee wore his formal gray uniform, while Grant arrived in an unbuttoned overcoat and mud-splattered boots. In that moment, Grant quickly wrote out the surrender conditions. The generosity of Grant towards the Southerners was perhaps the main reason the war did not continue. Grant noticed that Lee was staring at his own sword. Grant then decided that the Southern officers did not have to surrender their swords, as was customary. Grant also let the Southern soldiers keep their side-arms (pistols), their personal horses, and their baggage. In addition, Grant gave Union rations to the Southerners, who had no food.

After the signing of the documents, Lee sadly mounted his horse, Traveler. Grant stepped outside and saluted Lee, as did all of the Union officers. Lee raised his hat in return and rode off. Grant was extremely generous to the Southerners, but the Southerners still had to stack their muskets and surrender their cannons, and swear an oath of allegiance to the Union. Sporadic fighting continued in Texas until May.

Upon learning of Lee's surrender, C.S.A. President Jefferson Davis escaped and issued a call for all Southerners to engage in guerilla warfare in the Appalachian Mountains. (Guerilla warfare means to strike an enemy and then to run and hide). But there were no Southern newspapers left to publish Davis' letter, the Appalachians had many pro-Union people, and respected Southerners like General Lee completely opposed this idea. Davis was arrested May 10 and imprisoned for a time in leg irons. Many Northerners wanted to hang Davis, but President Andrew Johnson later proclaimed unconditional amnesty for him, and Davis was never convicted.

THE ASSASSINATION OF ABRAHAM LINCOLN

Five days after Lee's surrender and just over one month after Lincoln's second inauguration, a Southern actor conspired with others and then shot Abraham Lincoln on Good Friday, April 14, 1865. Lincoln was attending a play at Ford's Theatre in Washington, D.C., when his bodyguard John Parker left his post to get a drink at a nearby tavern. John Wilkes Booth snuck behind the president, aimed his .44–caliber gun inches from the back of Lincoln's head, and fired. President Lincoln was carried across the street to a nearby inn and died nine hours later.

After the assassination, Booth jumped to the stage below, shouted, "Sic semper tyrannis" ("Thus be it ever to tyrants"), and escaped on his waiting horse. Soon after, Federal soldiers trapped him in a barn, set it on fire, and a cavalryman shot Booth as he tried to escape. Lincoln's conspirators had planned to murder a number of Republicans, but failed in their attempts. Four of Booth's conspirators, three men and one woman, were hanged. Three others received life sentences, and one went to jail for six years.

Lincoln's assassination immortalized the 16th President, alongside Washington and Jefferson, as one of America's greatest heroes, and it led Congress to punish the South for its rebellion. The morning after Lincoln's murder, Walt Whitman wrote the poem "O Captain, My Captain." This poem expressed the grief many people in the North felt after Lincoln's death.

In Lincoln's second inaugural address, given a little over a month before his assassination, he stated:

> *With malice toward none; with charity for all; with firmness in the right, as God gives us to see the right, let us strive on to finish the work we are in; to bind up the nation's wounds; to care for him who shall have borne the battle, and for his widow, and his orphan— to do all which may achieve and cherish a just and lasting peace among ourselves, and with all nations.*

Lincoln had planned generous peace terms for Southerners who had joined the Confederate States of America, but his assassination gave control of the government to the Radical Republicans, who wanted to completely change the South.

CHAPTER 66

WINNERS, LOSERS, AND LASTING CHANGES

The three greatest winners of the war were the United States of America, the former slaves of the South, and American exceptionalism. The nation remained united, and there has never again been a serious call for secession. Although the war did not begin with the North fighting for the freedom of slaves, it became a primary goal of President Lincoln and the Republicans. After the Emancipation Proclamation in 1863, Maryland and Missouri began to free their slaves, Congress repealed the Fugitive Slave Law, and Congress passed and the Northern states adopted the 13th Amendment, ending slavery. The promises and ideals of the founding of our country, that all men are created equal, were more fully realized 89 years after its beginning.

The greatest losers of the war were the Confederate States of America, the slaveholders, and the non-slave holding Southern whites. The government of the C.S.A. ceased to exist. Slaveholders lost their most valuable possessions – their slaves – and the Southern economy was completely demolished after the war. Historian James McPherson wrote, "By 1865, the Union forces had…destroyed two-thirds of the assessed value of Southern wealth, two-fifths of the South's livestock, and one quarter of her white men between the ages of 20 and 40. More than half the farm machinery was ruined, and the damages to railroads and industries were incalculable…Southern wealth decreased by 60 percent."

Some Americans have adopted the Lost Cause Myth. This is the idea that Southerners formed the C.S.A. to primarily fight for states' rights and to further the cause for which the American Founding Fathers fought. Believers in the Lost Cause argue that Southerners would have gotten rid of slavery on their own and that Southern society was noble, just, and good. Writers have mythologized the pre-war South, and novels such as Gone with the Wind have done much to spread great historical inaccuracies.

There is nothing to suggest that Southerners would have gotten rid of slavery on their own. Each Southern state constitution stated that slavery would never end. The C.S.A. Constitution forbade any state from emancipating its slaves and stated that whites were the superior race to blacks.

The Founding Fathers fought for independence from Great Britain, representative democracy, and the ideal that all men are created equal, while at the same time defending the right to own another person. The existence of slavery in the birth country of the modern world's first republic is one of the greatest paradoxes of American history. Historian Michael Allen writes:

> *The Constitution legalized slavery through the 3/5 compromise and fugitive slave clause. The 13th, 14th, and 15th amendments were necessary to undo that. True, the Constitution does not state "slavery," but it says "persons in bondage." The Declaration of Independence is anti-slavery. Thus, the 13th-15th amendments made the Constitution be faithful to the Declaration of Independence, after nearly 100 years.*

The United States of America emerged from the Civil War a different country. Slavery was abolished and over 3 million Americans had freedom for the first time, the ideas of the supremacy of the states and secession were completely defeated, much of the South had been destroyed by the North, and the U.S. government was many times larger than it ever had been. Most significantly, the ideals of the nation as stated in the Declaration of Independence were more fully realized than ever in the U.S. Constitution. The United States had greatly changed, but the structure the American Founding Fathers established would continue to guide the nation throughout the remainder of the 1800s, the 1900s, and into the 21st century.